FRENCH FOUNDATIONS

Master the Basics in Two Weeks

Olly Richards

Copyright © 2017 Olly Richards Publishing

All rights reserved. No part of this publication may be reproduced, distributed or transmitted in any form or by any means, including photocopying, recording, or other electronic or mechanical methods, without the prior written permission of the publisher, except in the case of brief quotations embodied in critical reviews and certain other non-commercial uses permitted by copyright law. For permission requests, write to the publisher:

Olly Richards Publishing

olly@iwillteachyoualanguage.com

Trademarked names appear throughout this book. Rather than use a trademark symbol with every occurrence of a trademarked name, names are used in an editorial fashion, with no intention of infringement of the respective owner's trademark.

The information in this book is distributed on an "as is" basis, without warranty. Although every precaution has been taken in the preparation of this work, neither the author nor the publisher shall have any liability to any person or entity with respect to any loss or damage caused or alleged to be caused directly or indirectly by the information contained in this book.

French Foundations: Master the Basics in Two Weeks

Free Audio Download!

The best way to take advantage of this book is by listening to the free audio recordings that accompany every single written example of French you will find in the book.

To access the *Audio Vault*, visit the following link and create your free account today:

http://www.iwillteachyoualanguage.com/frenchbookaudio

Other Books by Olly Richards

French Short Stories for Beginners

German Short Stories for Beginners

Italian Short Stories for Beginners

Italian Short Stories for Beginners Vol 2

Russian Short Stories for Beginners

Spanish Short Stories for Beginners

Spanish Short Stories for Beginners Vol 2

English Short Stories for Intermediate Learners

Italian Short Stories for Intermediate Learners

Spanish Short Stories for Intermediate Learners

For more information visit:

http://iwillteachyoualanguage.com/amazon

Table of Contents

Introduction 7
How to Use This Book 13

Part 1: Getting Started with French
Chapter 1 - Getting Started 16
Chapter 2 - The Benefits of Learning French 20
Chapter 3 - Is French Hard to Learn? 26
Chapter 4 - A Linguistic Background to French 31

Part 2: French Pronunciation Guide
Chapter 5 - The Sounds of French 36
Chapter 6 - The French "R" 44
Chapter 7 - French Vowels 47
Chapter 8 - Reading and Pronouncing French 58
Chapter 9 - The Pronunciation of Words vs Phrases 65
Chapter 10 - How to Improve Your French Accent 74

Part 3: Mastering French Vocabulary - How to Memorise Any French Word You Need
Chapter 11 - Taking Advantage of What You Already Know 79
Chapter 12 - Choosing the Right Vocabulary 84
Chapter 13 - Remembering the Gender of French Words 86
Chapter 14 - Making Words Stick: How to Memorize French Vocabulary 88

Part 4: Tackling French Grammar
Chapter 15 - Nouns, Adjectives & Gender 100
Chapter 16 - Verb Conjugations Made Easy 111
Chapter 17 - Putting Sentences Together: Word Order 120
Chapter 18 - The French Past Tenses 125
Chapter 19 - Introducing the Subjunctive 130
Chapter 20 - French Prepositions 137

Part 5: Your French Learning Routine
Chapter 20 - Creating a Simple Learning Plan 144
Chapter 21 - Seven Mistakes to Avoid as a Beginner 156
Chapter 22 - Five Things to Get Right as a Beginner 161

Part 6: Appendices & Resources
Appendix 1 - Useful Words & Expressions................................172
Appendix 2 - Cognates..181
Appendix 3 - False Friends... 185
Appendix 4 - Verbs Using Être in the Perfect Tense................ 188
Appendix 5 - Irregular Subjunctive Verbs............................... 190

Introduction

Do you find that big changes in your life often originate from one single event? (Often an unhappy event.) This has always been the case for me. In fact, I can trace the story of my eight languages back to one, fateful day. It was a painful day, to be sure, but I would not have it any other way.

Let me explain. I was 19 years old and had just completed the first year of music college, where I was studying jazz piano. I had decided to take a year out from formal study, and had this rather silly plan that I would do nothing but practice the piano for the whole year and become the best pianist in the world! My girlfriend of two years had other ideas, however, and she decided that we should break up.

Being only 19, I did not take the breakup very well and some painful months ensued. However, everything that was to happen next, beginning with my buying a one-way Eurostar ticket to Paris, learning French in just a few months, traveling the world, and picking up seven other languages along the way, would never have taken place were it not for her decision.

I found myself in a tricky spot, having arranged for a "gap year", but feeling too sorry for myself to focus on what I had planned to do - practising the piano - which would have involved sitting on my own in a practice room for eight hours a day. Instead, I decided to take a job in a café in Central London in an effort to take my mind off things.

The job itself was far from glamorous. However, from the very first day, I realised I had unwittingly put myself in an exciting situation. You see, my colleagues in the café were from all overseas; mostly from European countries such as Italy, Sweden, Spain and France. Being in Central London, many of my customers were also from abroad. I began to learn cultural idiosyncrasies that intrigued me. For example, when a Spanish person orders "a coffee", what they want is an espresso, not a long black coffee. *("Why would anyone order such a small drink?")*

As time went by, I learnt about my colleagues' countries of origin. They missed home, of course, and would often tell me in detail about the things they missed: the beaches, the mountains, the great weather, the even-better food. I began to think: *"What must it be like to grow up in such wonderful places?"* Before long, that question had become: *"What if I could learn some French or Italian? Then I could go to these places too!"*

What started off as a terrible event, actually gave me the opportunity to meet people who would open my eyes to the rest of the world, expose me to different languages, and lead me to develop an insatiable passion for discovering more about them and their cultures.

Perhaps the most important detail about the events in that café was my reaction to hearing the many languages spoken by my colleagues: I felt stupid that I could only speak English. You see, it was not just the fact that my colleagues all spoke English. Many of them could speak each other's languages too. One German girl was equally comfortable chatting away in French, English, Spanish or Italian. I was stunned. How was this possible? I wanted to know. I *had* to know.

In all honesty, I am not sure whether it was the prospect of discovering the world, or the lingering pain of the break up, that led me to do what I did next. Perhaps it was a combination of the two things. Regardless, there was no stopping me. I did what any irrational 19-year-old would do: I quit my job in the café, left my flat and bought a one-way ticket to Paris. In Paris, I had no job waiting for me. I had no place to stay. I did not even speak French! It was silly, really, but I suppose it is the kind of thing you can get away with when you are a teenager, with nothing much to lose, and a healthy disregard for common sense. I needed to get away from the pain I was still feeling back home, and go somewhere I could feel less trapped in the "English bubble" I was becoming increasingly aware of.

Soon after arriving in Paris, I got a job in an international youth hostel in the beautiful Montmartre district in the North of the city, working at reception. I worked night shifts, which gave me plenty of free time that I used to study French by myself. One day, a French man walked past and popped his head through the open window. He was learning English, and wanted to know if I was learning French. *"Oui !"* I replied. He suggested meeting and practising our languages together. It was a novel idea for me, but I liked it, and agreed without hesitation. His name was Luca.

Luca and I began to meet regularly - two to three times per week. Each time we met, we would spend one hour speaking French and one hour speaking English. Within just a few weeks, the impact on my French was mind-blowing:

- I stopped worrying about making mistakes, because I was practising with someone I knew and trusted

- I no longer had to rely on impromptu conversations with strangers on the street to practise speaking French

- My confidence soared, as I had regular time to sit and practise my conversation skills

- I could easily try out all the vocabulary and grammar I was learning from my textbook

- Any questions or doubts about French were answered immediately

I later learnt that this activity is known as a *language exchange* or *tandem*, and language exchanges have since become an integral part of my approach to learning new languages, as they quickly allow me to develop the requisite confidence to start speaking with confidence.

While I hesitate to label anything a "shortcut" in language learning, there are undoubtedly shorter and longer paths to fluency. To put it more bluntly: Some activities help you to improve quickly, while others can easily waste your time. Learning to spot what helps, and what does not, is the most important skill for any language learner to develop.

The difficulty you face as a novice language learner, though, is that you do not yet have a clear idea of what works for you. You may begin, like I did, by simply picking up a French textbook and opening it on page one. The problem you quickly encounter, of course, is that there is a lot to learn. At this stage, the question shifts to become: What is the best way to learn all this information? When is a good time to start speaking? How can I avoid freezing up and forgetting the vocabulary I have learnt?

The good news, and what I have discovered through learning my eight languages, is that communicating well in French can be done with a relatively small knowledge of the language. While eliminating every last mistake, speaking with word-perfect grammar, and developing native-like fluency in French may take many years, the more modest (yet potentially life-changing) goal of holding confident, enjoyable conversations can be achieved in just a few months.

Uncovering the shortest path to learning French, therefore, is the basis of this book. I wanted to create for you the kind of book I wish I had when I was starting to learn French all those years ago - a no-nonsense guide, derived from real-world experience, that explains everything you need to know as a beginner in a simple and understandable way.

This book has been carefully organised into thematic chapters that will introduce you to the main concepts you need to tackle when learning French. We will look at different approaches to learning, the nuts and bolts of French vocabulary and grammar, how to tackle specific elements of French and other inspirations to help you along the way. You will tackle the key things you need to know to get started in French and the big challenges that often hold learners back.

Far from being a prescriptive book on *how* to learn the French language, my aim is give you all the concrete linguistic information you need, while also inspiring, provoking and challenging you to reflect on your own personal journey to learn French, which will ultimately lead you understand how you learn best. My goal is to make the process of learning French as simple and manageable as possible for you, so you can get on with the tantalising task of actually learning the language, and creating the life you desire, with the beautiful French language firmly at the centre.

For further inspiration as you read this book, you make like to visit my website, where I publish new articles every week dedicated to smart, effective language learning. If you like audio, you may also enjoy my podcast where I discuss language learning, and answer questions from learners around the world:

Blog: http://iwillteachyoualanguage.com

Podcast: http://iwillteachyoualanguage.com/podcast

Remember, you have access to free audio recordings of every example of French in the book. To access the Audio Vault, please visit:

http://www.iwillteachyoualanguage.com/frenchbookaudio

Bonne chance!

Olly

How to Use This Book

The core aim of French Foundations is to help you learn beginner's French quickly by providing a complete overview of the main features of the French language, along with insightful advice from the author about the best way to learn the information in each chapter. By the end of the book, you will have a grasp of French that might otherwise take many months to develop in regular weekly classes.

As such, French Foundations is quite different from a normal textbook. In a typical language textbook you would be presented with new grammar and vocabulary, followed by a series of exercises which are intended to help you practice what you have just learnt. In French Foundations, however, there are no written exercises, nor are you asked to learn or memorise anything while reading. Your aim should be simply to read the book from beginning to end, absorbing the information, noticing the features of the French language and how it differs from English.

By learning in this way, rather than getting bogged down in minutiae and waiting for months to learn essential concepts, you instead gain a complete picture of how French works *from the beginning*, which frees you up to learn independently and master the nuances of French in a more natural way. The book is structured in two main parts:

- The first part of the book is *input* – teaching you French grammar, vocabulary, pronunciation, etc.

- The second part of the book is *guidance* – teaching you *how* to study French and avoid common mistakes

Both parts of the book are equally important, as one without the other will lead to failure!

If you are looking to improve specific areas of your French, feel free to dip in and out of the book using the table of contents as a guide. If you are new to French, however, here is my suggested procedure for reading French Foundations:

1. Read the book once from cover to cover, without attempting to memorise anything. (You will, however, find that some parts stick in your memory naturally, which is an interesting phenomenon to observe!)

2. As you read, listen carefully to the accompanying audio for each example, which is indicated in square brackets throughout, e.g. [5.1]. The audio is freely available in the Audio Vault: http://www.iwillteachyoualanguage.com/frenchbookaudio

3. I recommend trying to complete the book within a relatively short space of time (10-14 days) specifically in order to avoid the temptation of entering "study mode". You might like to aim to read for 30 minutes each day, for example. The book has been kept to a manageable length in order to encourage you to do this!

4. After you finish the book, go back to specific areas of the book which you feel are important, and re-read

them. Alternatively, go back to the beginning and read the entire book for a second time. This time, you might like to commit some of the more important grammar, words or phrases to memory, and you will find guidance for doing this in the book.

Throughout the book there are a number of resources to help you:

- "Olly's Tip" – these are tips from me about my own experience of learning French and other languages. It is easy to get bogged down in specific details of learning French, and these sections are a friendly reality check to help keep you motivated and learning efficiently.

- Appendices – at the back of the book is an extensive resource section that includes expanded examples of key points from the book, such as useful phrases and important verbs to learn. You may be used to ignoring the appendices in other books – please do not ignore these ones, however, as they contain the most useful examples of French of all!

I hope you enjoy the book and find it to be a valuable learning experience!

Part 1: Getting Started with French

Chapter 1 - Getting Started

Are you one of those people who, when faced with a new challenge, just dives in and gets started? Or are you a pathological planner? We are always taught that planning is central to any well-defined aim. But I have always found that planning is only effective if you are well-informed enough to make a good plan in the first place. Self-evident? Perhaps, but vitally important.

The way you will become a proficient French speaker is through *lived experience.* Mastering a new language is not simply the result of learning large amounts of vocabulary and grammar rules, as our experiences from school would suggest. You could set out to memorise the entire contents of every French grammar book, but it would count for very little until you started to spend time with native speakers and had to put it all into practice.

So, if learning to speak French is the result of lived experience, then how exactly do you plan for this? After all, you cannot plan for what you have not yet experienced. As a novice language learner, it is very difficult to anticipate what you will learn from speaking French out in the real world. Therefore, planning for this "unknown" is hard, if not impossible. You could put together an intricate plan for how you will:

- Learn 1,000 words in French

- Master all irregular verbs in the present and past tenses

- Read a French novel cover-to-cover

However, experience tells me that you would probably give up after a couple of weeks, because these kinds of arbitrary goals simply do not translate into anything meaningful. Take the first goal of learning 1,000 words, for example:

- Why 1,000 words?

- Where would you choose these words from?

- How do you know you will ever need those words in conversation?

How about a goal such as: *"I want to become conversational in French in six months?"* Well, while this is a great *aspiration* to have, it is unhelpful as a *goal*, because unless you have learnt languages successfully before, you are unlikely to know exactly how to reach that goal.

Failing to plan, on the other hand, is no solution either. You will likely drift from one textbook to the next, lose yourself in YouTube videos, or even forget to study French for days at a time. Without a plan in place, you will wake up in two years' time no closer to your goal than when you started.

> "Would you tell me, please, which way I ought to go from here?"

> *"That depends a good deal on where you want to get to," said the Cat.*
>
> *"I do not much care where--" said Alice.*
>
> *"Then it does not matter which way you go," said the Cat.*
>
> *"--so long as I get SOMEWHERE," Alice added as an explanation.*
>
> *"Oh, you are sure to do that," said the Cat, "if you only walk long enough."*

(Alice's Adventures in Wonderland, Chapter 6)

So, in order to successfully learn French within a reasonable space of time, you need to have some idea of how you will do it. However, one certainty I can offer you from my years of language learning is this: the path to learning to speak French will be very different from how you may imagine it.

On your journey to fluency, you will have to contend with a range of emotions, from boredom to excitement, frustration to joy. Learning to pay attention to, and work with, these emotions, rather than letting them control you and your learning, will play a huge part in your success. If you can do this, along with paying attention to the learning methods that appear to be working well for you, you will gradually start to take control, and develop a language learning approach that works for you, rather than blindly following what other people recommend based on their own individual experience.

This is how you can learn French quickly. But enough of that. It is time to get started...

> *The journey of a thousand miles begins with one step.*
>
> - Lao Tzu

Chapter 2 - The Benefits of Learning French

Motivation Begins with Passion

In the introduction to this book, I told the story of my first encounter with foreign languages in the London café, and the painful breakup that led me there in the first place. What began as a terrible experience gave me an opportunity to meet new people and develop an interest in discovering more about them and their countries.

I had no idea how to learn a new language, and could not speak more than a couple of words in any. Fast-forward to today, and now I speak eight languages. What was responsible for this transformation?

Motivation.

I opened with this story because, whatever your background, whatever your level of experience, whether you think you have a talent for languages or not, your success learning French will not depend on these factors. The truth is that all successful language learners once started at the beginning, as complete beginners, wondering whether or not they had the ability to learn a foreign language. The one quality you can be sure all these learners had - before they became successful - was motivation. If you can foster a passion for French, if you can make it so important to you that it almost becomes your single defining purpose, if you can get clear on what it will mean to you to one day wake up and know that you are fluent in the language, then let me tell you, there is nothing that will stop you reaching that goal.

Having picked up this book on learning French, you have probably already thought about why you want to learn the language. It may help, though, to take a moment to be clear about these motives before moving on, and even write them down. Researchers have shown that those who write their goals down are far more likely to achieve those goals, and the best part is that it only takes a moment to do so.

I would like to propose a variation on the goal-setting exercise that can help you evoke your true feelings about French and why you wish to learn it. It can be a helpful exercise at the start of a language learning journey, but also at various points along the way, when you might be searching for motivation.

> *Close your eyes.*
>
> *You wake up, and you realise the hard work has paid off. You are now fluent in French after working hard at it for many months.*
>
> *Words roll off your tongue. You can express yourself effortlessly. You understand what others are saying to you.*
>
> *You "belong".*
>
> *How does it feel? What does it mean to you to have achieved this?*

Consider jotting down your response to this task in a notebook - it may have unexpected consequences in the future!

Becoming clear about your true motivation to learn French can have the power to transform your whole language learning journey. Your reason for learning French may be different from mine or from that of others reading this book. This motivation is personal to you and is the fuel that will power your journey to fluency in French. As tempting as it might be to skip ahead, it is important to stop and become clear on why you are learning the language first.

What Are the Benefits of Learning French?

Bearing all of this in mind, let's look at some of the main benefits that are available to everyone as a speaker of French. I encourage you to think about which of these benefits most motivate you and combine them with your own personal reasons for learning the language. You may well find some inspirations you had not yet considered!

Learning French Is Good for The Brain

It is widely accepted that there are several cognitive and physiological benefits associated with learning any second language and there are many advantages in choosing French specifically. It is estimated that over half the world's population uses more than one language on a daily basis and many monolingual English speakers, brought up speaking the global language of business and travel, are often not aware that this is quite normal. But in fact, in other parts of the world (including much of the French-speaking world) bilingualism is the norm.

Travel in France, Belgium, Switzerland, French Canada & Africa

France is the world's most popular destination for international tourists, regularly beating the US and China into second and third places respectively. Although people in common tourist areas in France have at least some level of English, many people have only limited English ability. When buying tickets, taking a train or eating in restaurants, you cannot rely on the locals being able to communicate in English and this means being able to speak French will greatly facilitate any trip to France, especially if you hope to explore the country independently.

Furthermore, being able to speak the local language will enable you to have much closer contact with the people you meet and will make your trip a much more enriching experience. This is also true in the French-speaking parts of Belgium and, to a lesser extent, Switzerland, although the latter country has a strong tradition of multilingualism and it is probably easier to find people who speak English there.

Communicate with People All Over the World

While French has long since been replaced by English as the global *lingua franca*, it is still widely spoken in many places all over the world in former French colonies, notably in large parts of Africa. It is estimated that globally, there are 110 million native speakers of French and that a further 190 million speak French as a second language. This means that learning French will equip you to communicate with large numbers of people worldwide.

Gain Advantages in Business

If you do business with French speakers, you will gain their respect by speaking their language. It was Nelson Mandela who said *"If you talk to a man in a language he understands, that goes to his head. If you talk to him in his language, that goes to his heart"*. Being able to conduct meetings and other business transactions in the native language of your partners without relying on English has a clear benefit, but simply being able to engage in small talk in French will have a dramatic effect on your relationship and command respect.

Gain a Deeper Understanding of French Culture

Language is intimately connected to culture and it is impossible to learn a language without learning about the culture of that country. France is a country with a proud cultural heritage and a long, fascinating history. It would be fair to say that the French are fiercely proud - and justifiably so - of their history and cultural heritage. The gateway to exploring this culture and that of other French-speaking countries is the French language. Of course, it is possible to appreciate French culture without speaking the language itself, but understanding French will give you a level of insight and personal satisfaction that is far more profound.

Open the Doors to French Art, Literature and Film

France is a country with a great tradition of art and literature. Reading novels or watching films in translation is nothing like experiencing them in the language in which they were written. Being able to understand French will open the doors to some of the world's great literary and artistic achievements.

The French have always excelled in the arts and this has continued into the modern era with important contributions to music and film. Every year, the Cannes Film Festival is one of the most anticipated events on the film industry calendar and showcases some of the world's most creative and progressive filmmaking. The Palme d'Or, the festival's most prestigious award, is awarded each year to an outstanding film from the festival.

For all these reasons, it is clear that choosing to learn French is a decision that will bring real and tangible benefits to your life. By now you are probably excited to get started, as all these benefits, and more, await you as you progress through this book and begin your journey to mastering French.

Chapter 3 - Is French Hard to Learn?

Somewhere down the line, French seems to have picked up a reputation for being a difficult language to learn, but in fact, once you overcome some of the initial unfamiliarity and begin to get a feel for the language, it is actually one of the easiest languages for English speakers to learn.

There is one single fact about French that makes it a relatively easy language for speakers of English to pick up and that is that the two languages share a huge amount of vocabulary. Learners who are just starting will find that many words in English are exactly the same as in French while others change only slightly, and the reason for this is that English has been borrowing from French for the best part of 1000 years.

Even better, many of these words are common, everyday words that you will use often. Here are a few examples:

[3.1]

- bus - bus

- table - table

- réservation - reservation

- responsable - responsible

(Note: Audio recordings of all French examples in this book are available to you in the Audio Vault. Just go to http://www.iwillteachyoualanguage.com/frenchbookaudio to access them!)

In recent years, the direction of borrowing has reversed and French has started absorbing English words in large numbers, much to the dismay of French purists and the *Académie Française*. This means that many modern words are also the same in French - although pronounced with a French accent. Here are some examples:

[3.2]

- email - email (purists insist on saying *couriel*, from *courier électronique*, 'electronic mail')

- sandwich - sandwich

- internet - internet

- week-end - weekend

There are many other French words and expressions that are familiar to English speakers and other words which are at various stages of being assimilated into English. Some examples might be *vin de table, c'est la vie, raison d'être, nom de plume* and many more.

Finally, there are some words which come from French and which have taken on a slightly new meaning in English. One example of this might be "chef". In French, the word *chef* actually means "boss" and the person in charge of a kitchen is the *chef de cuisine*. However, English-speaking kitchens and restaurants have retained the use of some French terms for positions such as *sous-chef*, *sommelier* and so on, and the term "chef" in English has now come to mean 'boss of the kitchen' instead of simply "boss".

The happy result of the close relationship of the two languages is that any English speaker taking up French starts off already knowing thousands of words that do not need to be learnt. So, one of the biggest tasks of learning a new language - acquiring new vocabulary - is considerably reduced! The proximity of French and English has created a problem, however, in that French and English share an unusually high number of *faux amis*, or false friends - words that look the same but have a different meaning. For example, *sensible* in French does not mean "sensible" but in fact means "sensitive". However, this presents no great problem, you will soon learn to spot these hidden traps.

There are certainly some other areas of French which are known to cause trouble for French learners, but none of them are quite as difficult as they seem. You may be aware that in French, nouns are considered either masculine or feminine and you may remember spending hours at school trying to memorise them. While in general, there is no way of telling from a noun whether it is masculine or feminine, there are some tips that will aid you in remembering, or failing that, at least enable you to have an educated guess. For example, almost all nouns ending in *-aison*, *-sion*, *-tion* or *-xion* are feminine while many nouns ending in a consonant are masculine. There are exceptions, of course, but these kinds of tips can help a student get started without being overwhelmed. Even if you get the gender of a noun wrong in conversation, you will see that it makes almost no difference and you will still be understood perfectly well! We will look at French word gender in more detail in Chapter 15.

Verbs are another challenge that any student of French will have to tackle, but just as with noun gender, learning verbs is not as difficult as some would have you believe. The important thing to know about French verbs is that they "inflect". That is, they change form depending on who is doing the action. Take a look at conjugations of the verbs *toucher* and *finir* below, for example:

[3.3 - 3.4]

toucher - to touch

- je touche - I touch
- tu touches - you touch
- il/elle touche - he/she touches
- nous touchons - we touch
- vous touchez - you (pl.) touch
- ils touchent - they touch

finir - to finish

- je finis - I finish
- tu finis - you finish

- il/elle finit - he/she finishes

- nous finissons - we finish

- vous finissez - you (pl.) finish

- ils/ells finissent - they finish

However, note that even though the spelling changes depending on the person doing the action, the pronunciation of all three forms is exactly the same which makes things a lot easier than it first might seem, at least when speaking.

You can hear how each of these forms is pronounced in the Audio Vault.

In addition to conjugating verbs, you will also have to learn how to put these verbs in different tenses, such as the past, present and future. However, the basic French tenses, while different from English, are not particularly challenging to understand. More good news is that some of the more 'complicated' tenses follow the same logic as English, meaning once you understand how to form the basic tenses, the more advanced tenses become simple to pick up.

In this book, I will explain all of the more difficult aspects of French one by one and show you why none of these things are as hard as they might seem at first.

Chapter 4 - A Linguistic Background to French

French is a member of the Romance family of languages and it is closely related to languages such as Italian and Spanish. It does not have as many native speakers as Spanish or Portuguese, but as previously mentioned, many millions of people around the world speak French as their first or second language.

Speakers of Romance languages usually find it very easy to learn others in the group due to similarities in grammar, vocabulary and other areas. Once you have learnt one of these languages, learning one or more of the others is greatly facilitated. If Romance languages can be considered brothers and sisters of French, then languages like English can be thought of as cousins. They are located further apart on the linguistic family tree but also have much in common.

Modern French is most closely related to the dialects that were spoken in the north of France, but due to France's influence and reach during the colonial period, it has gone on to become a truly global language. It is an official language in 29 countries worldwide as well as that of many international organisations, and is spoken not only in France but also Belgium, Switzerland, Canada, USA and many former French colonies in Africa. French was the global *lingua franca* from the seventeenth century until English became preferred in the years following World War II.

Let me introduce some of the key features of French.

1. Word Gender

As we noted in the previous section, French makes use of grammatical gender, meaning that nouns are considered either masculine or feminine. Whereas in English we use 'the' to introduce a noun, in French you will need to choose either *le* or *la* for masculine and feminine nouns respectively. Here are some examples ...

[4.1 - 4.2]

Masculine:

- le café - the café
- le supermarché - the supermarket
- le vin - the wine
- le poisson - the fish

Feminine:

- la terre - the earth
- la danse - *dance*
- la nourriture - food
- l'actrice - the actress

2. French Verb Tenses

Another difference between French and English is related to verbs. In English, verbs do not change their form much. In the present tense, the only variation is in the 3rd person (he/she) form, where an "s" is added:

- I say

- You say

- He/she says

- We say

- They say

However, in French, as we saw in the previous section, there are other changes, depending on who carries out the action.

French verb tenses (talking about events in the past, present or future) also differ somewhat from English. For example, when talking about the past, French essentially distinguishes between:

- An event that occurred just once at a single point in time, and

- Something that was true for an extended period of time or that happened regularly

English has an array of ways to express this, but in French it is much simpler, which means learners become accustomed to French tenses very quickly. In fact, it is probably much easier for English speakers to master French tenses than it is for French speakers to get to grips with the complicated tense system in English.

Another point to note is that, in French, use of the subjunctive is common. In English, this is a usage that has almost died out and is only present in expressions such as: *"It is important that we be on time"* (not *are* on time). However, not only the subjunctive is rarely needed at the beginner stages of French, but even when you do come to learn the subjunctive, you will discover that it often occurs in predictable places, and as part of common expressions, which will help you become accustomed to its usage quickly. Lastly, the French subjunctive is less complicated than Italian or Spanish, where it is used much more extensively.

French Pronunciation and Spelling

Some learners might have reservations about French pronunciation, although, again, there is nothing to be afraid of. There is only a handful of sounds that cause trouble for English speakers and they are not particularly difficult to produce with some practice. Perhaps the most notorious sound for English speakers is the French "r" as there is nothing similar in English phonology. It is pronounced in the back of the throat with the throat partially closed and is similar to the sound of clearing one's throat, only more delicate. More on this later in Chapter 6.

Another pitfall for English speakers is that French distinguishes between "u" and "ou" (as in *tu* and *vous*) whereas English only has the sound in "you", which is neither one nor the other. This can lead to some rather amusing situations as when you think you are saying "neck" (*cou*) you may actually pronounce *cul* - meaning "arse" - which could end up being rather embarrassing! Thankfully, most of the other vowels and consonants of French are much easier for English speakers to produce. In the next section, you will learn all about these sounds and how to master them, so do not worry about it too much right now!

One final area to highlight is French spelling, which may seem rather erratic at first sight. Like English, spoken French has gone through many changes since it was first written down, and these changes have not been matched by changes in the written language. The result is that French words now contain a number of letters that are no longer pronounced (as we will see in Chapter 8). Coupled with this is the array of accents and other markings (known as *diacritics*) above and below the letters which may, at first sight, make written French seem quite intimidating. You should not allow this to worry you, though, as there is nothing terribly difficult beyond a few idiosyncratic spellings to remember - and you can comfort yourself with the thought that...English spelling is much worse!

This section has given you an overview of some of the linguistic areas you can expect to find when you start learning French. We will look at all of these aspects in more detail as we continue, starting with French pronunciation.

Part 2: French Pronunciation Guide

Chapter 5 - The Sounds of French

An Introduction to French Pronunciation

Before talking specifically about French pronunciation, let's just remind ourselves of a very important point regarding the pronunciation of foreign languages in general. Unless you learn your second language from a very young age, it is almost impossible to ever achieve native-level pronunciation. Even for somebody who marries a person from a foreign country, moves to that country and lives there for twenty years, speaking that language every day, they will still speak with at least a hint of an accent. This being so, it is important for language learners to realise that speaking with a perfect accent is not a realistic objective and that however long you learn, the moment you open your mouth, people will probably know you are not a native speaker of the language.

There is a tendency among many students to expend too much energy on perfecting their pronunciation, which can actually slow their progress, and some may even develop a complex about their accent, which is unfortunate. It is important to remember that native-level pronunciation should not be your goal. Instead, you should focus on clear and intelligible pronunciation, and if you can accept this, then you have taken one more step toward acquiring a new language.

Most languages have alphabets and some, such as Spanish and Turkish, have alphabets where each letter corresponds exactly to one sound. This makes reading these alphabets easy, because each word sounds the way it is written. Speakers of other languages, such as English, are not so lucky. Think about words ending in "-ough." The words "cough", "though", "through", "bough" and "enough" are written the same way, but have five different pronunciations! Some sounds, like the common "th" sound in English, do not even exist in many other languages, which explains why French speakers learning English are prone to saying "one", "two", "tree". For English speakers learning French as a second language, things are no different. There are some entirely new sounds, and without mastering these sounds, your pronunciation can sound just as strange. However, this is not a cause for concern; it just requires practice. Think of it as like learning any other new skill, such as roller-skating. At the beginning, it feels very unnatural and you have to think carefully about every movement to make sure you do not fall over. When you start out, you feel clumsy and it might be quite difficult to stay standing. However, if you keep practising, you will soon be able to skate without consciously thinking about it at all. It is a bit like this when you learn to pronounce the sounds of a new language. At first, you have to concentrate on the sounds you are making, but very soon, you will start speaking naturally without having to think about it. Now let's take a more detailed look at the sounds of French.

Olly's Tip:

I have known many people who become self-conscious of their pronunciation in a foreign language. If you take a second to think of the many foreign movie stars, sportsmen or politicians you may have heard speak on TV or radio in English, I am sure you were much more interested in what they had to say than critiquing their accent!

In fact, it is more likely you found their foreign accent endearing, and nice to listen to. Try to keep this in mind as you move forward with your French, and especially if you have a tendency to worry about your pronunciation. The content of what you have to say is far more important!

The Basics of French Pronunciation - The Sounds of French

In order to even begin a serious discussion about pronunciation in any language, you must be aware that what you read and what you pronounce are not always the same, as we know is the case with English and French. To this end, there is a useful tool called the International Phonetic Alphabet (IPA) (https://en.wikipedia.org/wiki/International_Phonetic_Alphabet) that can be a useful reference. I do not recommend you learn the IPA at first, but if you do find yourself getting stuck with pronunciation, it might be a useful tool to explore, as it helps you focus clearly on the sound that is being used.

French Consonants

Let's start with the consonants. Many consonant sounds in French are almost identical to English, although if you listen very carefully you will hear that there are sometimes subtle differences. If you can train yourself to notice these differences and reproduce them yourself, your pronunciation will sound less foreign.

Take a look at the examples below and listen to the audio files to hear the pronunciation. (Click here to access the Audio Vault.)

[5.1 - 5.22]

- /b/ - bateau (like in the English word 'boat')
    - bon / good
    - beau / handsome
    - besoin / need
- /d/ - dîner (like in the English word 'dinner')
    - dans / in
    - donner / give
    - différent / different

- /g/ - gare (like in the English word 'gift')
    - général / general
    - gros / big
    - groupe / group
- /f/ - flic (like in the English word 'fall')
    - un film / film
    - fait / fact
    - faire / to do
- /l/ - lait (like in the English word 'lazy')
    - longtemps / long
    - leurs / their
    - loin / far
- /m/ - mêler (like in the English word 'mix')
    - mon / mine
    - merci / thank you
    - un monde / world

- /n/ - nous (like in the English word 'nice')

    - non / no

    - un nom / name

    - nouveau / new

- /s/ - sac (like in the English word 'sack')

    - Note: Always pronounced /s/ when beginning or ending a word as in "son" and "bonus," but /z/ when placed between two vowels, as in "nasal".

    - si / if

    - sans / without

    - besoin / need (pronounced /z/ in this word)

- /ʃ/ - chat (like in the English word 'machine')

    - Note: "ch" in French is always soft like the 'sh' in the English word 'shoot', not the 'ch' the English 'chocolate'.

    - une chose / thing

    - une chance / chance

    - chercher / to look for

- /v/ - vous (like in the English word 'vile')
    - voir / to see
    - vrai / true
    - vite / quick
- /z/ - zoo (like in the English word 'zoo')
    - Note: The letter "z" rarely appears at the beginning of a word. It often appears at the end, but in this case, it is usually silent. For example: nez / nose; assez / enough.
    - zéro / zero
    - magazine / magazine
    - bizarre / bizarre

There are also a few consonant sounds in French which are unique cases and not so common in English:

[5.23 - 5.28]

- /ʒ/ - japonais (rare in English, as in "treasure")
    - je / I
    - toujours / always
    - juste / right

- /ɲ/ - poignet (as in "nuke" or the "ñ" in "español" in Spanish")

- /ŋ/ - camping, smoking

    o   gagner / to win

In English, when these three consonants are stressed, they are *aspirated*. This means you blow out air when you make the sound. Try putting a small piece of paper on your hand, hold it next to your mouth and say 'paper' loudly. The paper moves, right? But in French, these sounds are not aspirated. Try making the same sound but without blowing any air so the paper on your hand does not move and you will be somewhere close to the French pronunciation.

All of the sounds we have looked at so far are different in French than in English, but not drastically so. There is, however, one infamous sound in French that has nothing even vaguely similar in English phonology and that is what we are going to look at next.

Chapter 6 - The French "R"

In French, there are really only two sounds that English-speakers need to work hard on from the beginning, and after which, the rest is just fine tuning! The first of these sounds is the French "r".

The French "r" sound has a fiendish reputation among English-speakers of French and, having no close equivalent in English, it is a sound that most people will need to practise. However, the first thing to remember is that there is no need to be intimidated by this sound - most people will be able to produce a passable imitation of the French "r" from the beginning and French speakers will be able to understand. After this, you will only improve with time.

The pronunciation of the French "r" varies from region to region, and sometimes even from speaker to speaker. It is nothing like an English "r" but it is not quite like a Spanish one either (which is almost a purring noise made by vibrating the tongue against the roof of the mouth). A French "r" comes from deeper within the throat and is a little similar to the sound made when clearing your throat - except softer and less harsh. To produce the correct sound, try to partially close the back of your throat, keeping your tongue in a neutral position and not touching the roof or your mouth, and blow air out from deep in your throat (again, almost as if you were trying to clear your throat). The best way to practise this is with a recording or, better, with a native French speaker, so you can listen to the sound you should be trying to reproduce.

[6.1 - 6.2]

- /R/ - rue
    - rien / nothing
    - dire / to say
    - très / very

Olly's Tip:

To really test your comfort level with the French "r" try saying words which contain the "r" alongside another consonant. For example:

- *pratiquer*
- *trier*

These are not at all like the English "consonant clusters". As mentioned before, try to approach the French "r" as a new sound, and not be influenced by the sound of the English "r". The two sounds may be represented by the same letter of the alphabet but they are completely different. Try saying the English words "prove" and "true" and notice how your lips are rounded to make the "r" sound. With the French "r", you should not round your lips in this way as the sound comes from your throat and not your lips.

Chapter 7 - French Vowels

The 12 French Vowels

Vowels are sounds produced with no obstruction to the air leaving the mouth, and you probably know vowels in English as five letters: a, e, i, o and u. Actually, there are many more than five vowel sounds in both English and French, and French is considered to have up to 13 vowels, although this can vary according to region and dialect.

Many of the vowels in French are similar to their corresponding vowels in English, but not identical. For pronunciation, this small difference in vowel sounds matters more than usual - if you try to speak French with "English vowels", you will sound very foreign!

Below, you will find the French vowels, together with English words where the sound of the vowel would be considered similar. Remember, the comparisons below are only approximations. While these English comparisons are helpful to get your bearings, you should listen carefully to these vowels with the accompanying audio recordings from the start, and imitate the sound you hear as closely as possible. Pay as much attention to the differences with the English vowel as to the similarities.

Let's start with the most common and simple vowel sounds in French:

[7.1 - 7.12]

- /a/ - *gars* (as in the English word car)
    - *pas* / not
    - *la* / the (feminine)
    - *avec* / with
- /e/ - fait (like the first part of 'way' in English)
    - beauté / beauty
    - déjà / already
    - désolé / sorry
- /i/ -vie / tree
    - fini / finished
    - appris / learnt
    - le midi / noon
- /o/ -beau (like English 'go' but with more rounded lips)
    - une eau / water
    - une info / a piece of information

- beaucoup / a lot

- /u/ - doux (like English "you" but with more rounded lips)

    - où / where
    - pourquoi / why
    - toujours / always

- /ɛ/ -tête (as in the English word head)

    - une bête / a beast
    - une fête / a party
    - être / to be

There are some vowels in French that have no real equivalent in English and thus require more attention. These sounds may take some time getting used to but the most important thing right now is just to be able to *hear* the differences. Listen to the recordings, notice the differences and do your best to imitate them:

[7.13 - 7.20]

- /ɑ/ - pâtes

    - This sound is extremely close to [a] above and some speakers do not distinguish between these two vowels, say it with the mouth wide

- o une tâche / task

- o un âge / age

- o une âme / soul

- /ø/ - œufs

    - o It is like "uh" but with the lips rounded, somewhere between 'er' and 'ooh'

    - o un voeu / wish

    - o un dieu / god

    - o mieux / better

- /œ/ - seul

    - o This is similar to the /ø/ sound but less rounded, closer to 'er' than 'ooh'

    - o un fleuriste / florist

    - o une peur / fear

    - o une heure / hour

- /ə/ - cela

    - o Again, this is similar to the previous sounds but with the mouth nearly closed

- regarder / to look at

- demain / tomorrow

- depuis / since

Olly's Tip:

When it comes to sounding "foreign" in a foreign language, it is often the vowels that give you away more than anything else. In English, we are extremely lazy when pronouncing vowels and usually mutter rather than articulate them clearly. For example, look of the word deliberately and how many vowels it contains. Now try saying the word aloud and ask yourself how many of the vowels are pronounced clearly? How difficult it would be for a learner of English to tell the difference between the vowels?

Because of our lazy vowels in English, we often transfer that laziness to our pronunciation of vowels in other languages. For this reason, it is especially important to pay close attention to the pronunciation of the vowels in French in order to refine your accent.

Ou vs. U

The second of the two sounds English speakers find most difficult is the "u" sound in *tu* as opposed to "ou" in *vous*. This sound presents far less of a challenge than the "r" sound and perhaps the greatest problem comes from the fact that many students do not realise these vowels are pronounced differently. Since English has no corresponding sound, if an English speaker sees *tu* or *vous* written on a page, they will probably pronounce them both to rhyme with "you". English "you" is closer to French *vous* although not exactly the same, but the sound is altogether different from *tu*. You will probably find, however, once this difference has been pointed out, the problem quickly evaporates with a little practice. Let's consider these two sounds:

[7.21 - 7.24]

- /u/ - doux - similar to English "you" but with the mouth more rounded and the sound stays constant

- /y/ - jus - produced like /u/, but as a front vowel, meaning the mouth is drawn back toward the tongue

    o salut / hi

    o une voiture / car

    o un truc / thing, thingy

A simple way to get a close approximation of this sound is to first make the "ou" sound in the English "you". Hold your lips in the same shape as for "you" but push your tongue further forward so that it is almost between your lips and try to make the "ou" sound. You will find that it is impossible to make this sound and the sound you are now making is, in fact, a French "u"! If you can practise a few words while listening to a recording, you will soon be able to master this sound. This vowel is extremely important, because without it, speakers will confuse very common words such as "tout" (all) with "tu" (you)!

The 4 French Nasal Vowels

The four nasal vowel sounds can also prove challenging because they are entirely new to English speakers. For example, the "n" sound that appears at the end of a word is not pronounced at all with the tip of the tongue, as in English. No contact is made between the tongue and the top of the mouth. Instead, air is released simultaneously from the nose and the mouth. It is very easy to know if you are pronouncing these correctly. Practice the vowels with a finger pressed against one side of your nose. You can feel a vibration!

Listen carefully to the recordings here and compare the nasalised and non-nasalised sounds.

[7.25 - 7.32]

- /ɛ/ - *vin*
    - (like "van" in English, but the key is to not "release" the /n/ at the end of the word)

- une main / hand
- maintenant / now
- une fin / end

- /õ/ - mon, son, ton
  - non / no
  - une question / question
  - un garçon / boy

- /ɑ/ - enfant, avant, devant
  - dans / in
  - quand / when
  - sans / without

- /œ̃/ - un / a, one
  - In some French-speaking regions this nasal vowel has merged with /ɛ̃/, but many speakers still distinguish it, so you should be aware of its existence.
  - brun / brown
  - aucun / none

- chacun / each

The 3 French Semi-Vowels

As you can see, French has quite a lot of different vowel sounds! Most French vowels produce a single sound but semi vowels start off as one sound and change into another one as you pronounce them. This may sound strange but it is something that exists in English as well, you just might not be aware you are doing it! In English, the effect can be seen in words like "wheel", but in French the change is subtler.

[7.33 - 7.38]

- /ɥ/ - huile

    - Try saying "we" and holding it and then move your tongue up to the top of your mouth. The sound you are trying to produce is the sound you make when you move your tongue. The change is subtler than in the English word "wheel"

    - tuer / to kill

    - depuis / since

    - une cuisine / kitchen

- /w/ - oust

    - Try saying "ooh" and holding it and then saying "west". The sound you make when you start saying "west" is the sound saying you are trying to make.

    - oui / yes

    - un whisky / whisky

    - un wagon / wagon

- /j/ - hier

    - Try making an "ee" sound and holding it and then saying "air". It is the sound you make at the moment you start saying "air".

    - un oeil / eye

    - une fille / girl

    - briller / to shine

The most important thing for now is to have a rough idea of each of the sounds of French. In the next few chapters, you will learn about reading and pronouncing French words and phrases. It is through practice reading and speaking in French that you will master the sounds of French so do not worry if you cannot remember them all or produce each one perfectly right now. It will come with time.

Olly's Tip:

Of all the sounds you need to master in French, the "r" and "u" are the only sounds that have the potential to cause communication problems, and leave your conversation partner scratching their head. (Or perhaps giggling depending on what you have just said!) Once you have mastered these two important sounds, the rest will fall into place with practice.

Chapter 8 - Reading and Pronouncing French

Even if you have never had any contact with the French language before, you will probably have noticed just from reading this book that French has a slightly eccentric spelling system! You may have seen, for example, that French contains many silent letters - letters that are written but not pronounced. There are a number of reasons for this being the case. Written French is based on the pronunciation of the spoken French of the 12th or 13th Centuries, and the forms used today have changed very little since the 17th century, when the written language was codified by the *Académie Française*.

As you might expect, the pronunciation of spoken French has changed a great deal since then! However, the written form has remained the same, which means there is now a considerable disparity between the written and the spoken forms. Coupled with this is the fact that when the language was codified, scholars changed the spellings of some words, deliberately adding silent letters to reflect Latin etymology. This did little to help make written French any easier to master! Many other European languages like German, Spanish or Italian do not contain all these extra letters. These are what we call "phonetic" languages, meaning you pronounce the letters as you see them and spelling tend to follow the rules. French, as we have seen, is not phonetic, and learners need to spend a little extra time understanding the written language.

Incidentally, English is also an extremely non-phonetic language for the same reasons as French. Written English was codified hundreds of years ago but the written form has not changed to reflect changes in pronunciation. English, too, is cursed with some of those unhelpful "Latinised" spellings in the same way as French. In the 14th Century when Geoffrey Chaucer wrote *The Knightes Tale* (*The Knight's Tale* in *The Canterbury Tales*), all the letters in "knightes" would all have been pronounced but in modern English, the "k" and the "gh" are silent and the "e" has been dropped. This is why in modern speech, "knight" is pronounced exactly the same as "night" and both rhyme with "site". The consolation you can draw from this - and the bad news for anyone learning English - is that the French spelling system is still more logical than the one we have in English, which is probably the most illogical of any of the world's major languages!

Most silent letters in French are final consonants which for one reason or another are not pronounced. As a general rule - but one which is, as ever, proven by numerous exceptions - the following letters are usually pronounced:

- -b
- -c
- -f
- -k
- -l
- -q
- -r

Take a look at the examples below and listen to the recordings:

[8.1]

- club*, pub* - club, pub
- aplomb - aplomb
- truc - thing
- blanc - white
- nocif - noxious
- cerf - stag
- genial - great
- gentil - kind, nice

The following consonants are usually silent:

- -d
- -g
- -p
- -s
- -t
- -x
- -z

Listen and notice the differences between the recording and the written words. In each case, you will first hear a word where the final consonant is silent, then an exception in which it is pronounced:

[8.2]

- laid - ugly
- sud - south
- beaucoup - much, many, lots of
- slip* - underpants
- filet - net
- short* - shorts (item of clothing)
- choix - choice
- dix - ten
- chez - at (somebody's house)
- fez* - fez (type of hat)

*Note that in French, many of the exceptions are due to the word being borrowed from another language - as these examples demonstrate.

Olly's Tip:

When you are a beginner in a new language, most native speakers are extremely forgiving of mistakes. However, when I first learnt French, the mistake that would most reliably produce a laugh from a French person was to pronounce the final consonant in a word where it should be silent. I remember saying the word loup (wolf) as the English "loop", with a hard "p", and my friend almost collapsing on the floor with laughter. Needless to say, this was not a welcome reaction!

As a result, I developed a personal rule of thumb that any consonant at the end of a word in French should not be pronounced! This is not a universal rule, but it is correct more often than not, and I found it much better than the alternative. When in doubt, and to save your blushes, avoid hard consonants at the end of words!

Some words contain silent consonants within the word, usually due to the additions made to "Latinised" words, as mentioned above: *sept*, "seven", where the "p" is silent.

The "e" in French can be a little confusing at first because it has several different uses and can also carry all of the French accents. The French "é" and "è" can almost be considered as separate letters as they have their own phonetic sound. With an "ê", the accent does not change the pronunciation but usually indicates that the "e" was once followed by an "s" that has since disappeared. Sometimes, but not always, English has retained the "s" where French has discarded it, for example: *crête*, "crest". An "e" with no accent can be silent or it can change the pronunciation of the preceding letters, as in English: think of English "pin" and "pine". An example from French might be *lourd*, *lourde*, the masculine and feminine forms of the word for "heavy". In the masculine form, the "d" is silent but in the feminine form, it is pronounced.

A final -x often indicates a plural form that has replaced an -s from an older form of French: *cheval*, *chevaux* ("horse", "horses") or *château*, *châteaux* (castle, castles). The "x" in these words is normally silent unless said in conjunction with other words - more on this later.

An important group of words containing silent letters is verbs. I mentioned in the section on verbs that *regarde*, *regardes* and *regardent* are all pronounced exactly the same, *finis* and *finit* are the same, as are *vends* and *vend*, and that the -ent in *vendent* and *finissent* are silent. One other important spelling idiosyncrasy to pay attention to is a small group of words that have pronounced letters in the singular but which become silent in the plural: *œuf*, *œufs* - "egg", "eggs". In the singular, the "f" is pronounced but not in the plural.

If all this sounds too complicated, there is really nothing to worry about. Learners of French soon become accustomed to all this strangeness and you will soon be able to avoid traps set for novices: you will know, for example, that *mont Blanc* has neither a "t" nor a "c" when you pronounce it correctly. And remember, English is so much worse!

Olly's Tip:

The best way to avoid letting your English pronunciation interfere with your French is to spend a lot of time listening to audio. The Audio Vault *that comes with this book is a great start, but whatever material you study with in the future, look for resources that come with accompanying audio, so you can train your ear to hear the sounds of French, and mimic what you hear. With a mix of exposure, attention and time, you will find yourself developing a good accent naturally... but it all starts with listening!*

Chapter 9 - The Pronunciation of Words vs Phrases

For beginners learning French, there is one aspect of French vocabulary that may, at first glance, complicate matters: homophones. Homophones are words that have different meanings but are pronounced or spelt the same. In English, an example of this might be "coach" which can mean either a sports trainer or a large type of vehicle.

In French, one example is *ou* and *où* meaning "or" and "where" respectively, and another example is *est* meaning "is" and *et* meaning "and". Someone starting out learning French might reasonably ask the question: *if two words sound identical, how can you tell which one the speaker means?*

In reality, this is the kind of problem you might worry about in theory, but not in practice. The reason is that the *context* of what is being said will reveal all. Consider our last example in English. How do you know which "coach" a person is talking about? From the context of the sentence, the meaning is almost always completely unambiguous. For example, if a person says they will be traveling by coach, we know the person is talking about a vehicle since that is what we use to travel. If somebody says their coach told them to go running every day, we know it is their trainer we are talking about since vehicles cannot speak. In fact, English is littered with homophones and they almost never give us trouble. In this example sentence, we know that the word "trainer" means "sports coach" and not "sports shoe" because that is what makes sense in the conversation. It is the same in French.

Let's take another example. In French, *sang* ("blood"), *cent* ("one hundred") and *sans* ("without") are all pronounced exactly the same but if we hear someone say *il était couvert de sang* we know it means "he was covered in blood" since "one hundred" or "without" make absolutely no sense in this sentence. The only possibility is "blood". You will quickly find that you do not need to mentally search through a list of words to compare the various possibilities before you understand that the subject, the sentence and the context will all help you work out what is going on. You will instinctively know, as you do in English, providing, of course, that you know all the different meanings of the word.

Sometimes the grammar can help too. Masculine and feminine nouns can sometimes give you a clue. *La foi* ("faith") and *le foie* ("liver") are homophones but the first is feminine and the second is masculine so you know if someone is talking about *ma foi*, they are talking about their faith while if they say *mon foie*, they are referring to their liver. Even in a sentence where the gender is not specified like *je n'ai pas de foi*, you know the person is saying they have no faith since if they had no liver, they would not be standing there talking to you!

Just as in English, homophones can give rise to clever wordplay and can be the source of humour. *Plutôt* means "rather" but *plus tôt* means earlier, which could give rise to a sentence like *je préfère y aller plutôt plus tôt que plus tard* meaning "I rather prefer to go earlier rather than later". *Ver* ("worm"), *vert* ("green") and *verre* ("glass") are all homophones which means you could end up saying *j'ai un ver vert dans mon verre* ("I have a green worm in my glass") which might be quite hard to understand - but you could clarify by saying *ver de terre*, "earthworm", to avoid confusion. In French, as in any language with homophones, if there is any doubt as to the meaning, a speaker would normally think of another way to phrase it so as to make it more easily comprehensible.

Olly's Tip:

Sometimes, language problems are only a problem in theory. One of the advantages of learning many foreign languages is getting to know which aspects of the language learning process are worth allowing yourself to worry about, and which you can relax about. Homophones is one example of a language learning problem that can cause you to feel overwhelmed and confused. "How am I ever going to learn all these words when they sound identical?"

With experience, however, you learn to simply not worry about any hypothetical confusion that might arise, and instead trust that the context of your conversations will make it clear what word is being used.

Liaison: Stringing the Words Together

The final point to be aware of in French pronunciation is *liaison*. Put simply, liaison is when words are strung together in speech, such that they end up sounding like one (very) long word. This happens when the consonant at the end of one word meets a vowel at beginning of the following word, resulting in the two words effectively being joined together.

Now, as we have seen, many French words have consonants at the end which are silent. However, if one of these silent consonants is combined with a vowel at the start of the following word, it will often need to be pronounced. For example, when the French word *les*, the plural form of "the", is pronounced alone, the "s" is silent. However, if you say *les animaux* (the animals) the words join together and the "s" is pronounced as a "z" sound, giving something like "lezanimaux" (remember, the "x" at the end is silent).

Here are some examples of some word endings that change their pronunciation with liaison:

[9.1 - 9.4]

Words Ending -s

- les hommes* /lez- ɔm/ - the men

    o *the "h" in hommes is silent

- vous avez /vuz- ave/ - you have

- Les États-Unis /lez- etaz- yni/ - The United States

- o Note: There are two liaisons here

- deux idées /døz- ide/ - two ideas

Words Ending -n

- mon ami /mõn- ami/ - My friend
- un homme /ɛ̃n- ɔm/ - a man
- arriver en avance /aʁive ɑ n- avɑ s/ - to arrive on time

Words Ending -x

- faux amis /foz- ami/ - false friend
- six idées /siz- ide/ - six ideas
- aux Etats-Unis /oz- etatsyni/ - in the United States

Words Ending -t

- tout à fait /tut- a fɛ/ - absolutely, completely
- tout à coup /tut- a ku/ - all of a sudden
- tout à l'heure /tut- a lœʁ/ - just now

We can say that with liaison, there are three possibilities:

1. Cases where words must be joined in this way
2. Cases where words cannot be joined

3. Cases where it is optional

There are rules that govern when liaison can and cannot be used, but these are not so helpful at this stage. Instead, we will illustrate these cases with some examples.

[9.5 - 9.6]

Obligatory Liaison

- Mes amis /mez- ami/ - My friends
- Nous avons /nuz- avõ/ - we have
- États-Unis /etaz- yni/ - United States (USA)

Impossible Liaison

- Un homard - a lobster
- Mes amis ont dit - my friends said (no liaison between *amis* and *ont,* there is liaison between *mes* and *amis*)

Note the difference between *un homme* ("a man") and *un homard* ("a lobster"). The difference is due to the fact that the "h" in *homard* is considered to be "aspirated" whereas the "h" in *homme* is "silent". These terms are slightly misleading as the "h" in *homard* is not aspirated as in English and is pronounced (or *not* pronounced, to be more accurate) exactly the same as the "h" in *homme* in isolation - the difference is that a silent "h" allows liaison but an aspirated "h" does not allow it. There is no way to tell if an "h" is aspirated or not and each word must be learnt.

In other cases, the decision of whether to use *liaison* is up to the speaker, although in some cases it is more common than in others. In general, using more liaison marks more careful, formal speech and using less liaison marks more informal, colloquial speech.

[9.7 - 9.8]

Optional Liaison

These sentences would almost always be pronounced with liaison:

- Chez un ami (shay-Zunami) - At a friend's house

- Vous êtes allés /vuz- ɛt(z) ale/ - You went

- Vous aussi /vu(z)- osi/ - you too

Liaison in the following sentences is more optional, and would mark more careful, formal speech:

- Trop amusant /tʁo(p) amyzɑ/ - too funny, too amusing

- Il y est allé /il i ɛ(t) ale/ - He went there

- ils vont à l'école /il vɔ̃(t) a lekɔl/ - They are going to school

The advice for you as a learner is, as ever, not to fret about this! The best way to learn liaison and any other features of French pronunciation is to train your ear to listen carefully to the pronunciation of native speakers and to copy them. You will soon instinctively know when you need to use liaison and when you cannot. From the beginning, you will learn to say *nous avons* with liaison and will repeat the correct pronunciation automatically. You may get caught out pronouncing words like *les haricots* ("the beans") with liaison when it is actually not possible since the "h" in *haricots* is aspirated, but even if you do this, the reality is that it does not matter! What you say will still be perfectly understandable. Console yourself with the fact that sometimes even native French speakers make mistakes and need to check the dictionary to see if an "h" is aspirated or silent!

Olly's Tip:

Liaison sounds really complicated when you read it on paper, but as long as you are listening to French, I guarantee it will come very naturally to you! You will pick it up very quickly as your brain gets used to the sound and flow of the French.

Chapter 10 - How to Improve Your French Accent

We have already looked in detail at French pronunciation, so now let's consider how you can apply everything you have learned and start to improve your *accent*.

For a start, what is the difference between pronunciation and accent? Are they not the same?

Pronunciation is the way the individual sounds of a language are produced. In order to be understood, you need to pronounce words correctly. You might not sound like a native speaker but if you have good pronunciation, you will be able to pronounce all the language sounds and words clearly and understandably. An accent, on the other hand, is a way of pronouncing words that differs by region, country or social group. As a French learner, you will naturally speak with a foreign accent at first, but the better your accent is the more "native like" you will sound. Perfecting your French accent is difficult, but it can certainly be improved with the right approach.

This chapter will be of interest if you have ever found yourself wondering:

- Is my accent any good?

- Do I sound too "foreign"?

- What I can do to improve my accent?

Let's start with some perspective.

A Lot of Listening!

An eight-year-old Japanese girl called Natsuko once came to take guitar lessons with me. She had recently moved to the UK, and spoke no English whatsoever. As you might expect from a child of that age, after just one year attending school in her new country she spoke excellent English, and had a nice rounded British accent to boot! I saw Natsuko every Tuesday throughout her first year at school, and watching her transformation was a special experience.

At the beginning, since Natsuko could not speak English, her only option was to do nothing but listen to the English she heard around her and try to discover what was going on. How much time do you imagine she would have spent listening to English during that year at school? Assuming six-hour school days, a smattering of after-school activities and six weeks of school holidays, I estimate she spent about 1,500 hours listening to English during her first year.

Now, if an eight-year-old child needs 1,500 hours of exposure to a new language in order to develop native-like pronunciation in the language, it is likely that we, as adults, need at least that, if not more. After all, Natsuko had the benefit of teachers and classmates supporting her all-day long. In your case, let's be generous and say you would need to amass around 2,000 hours of meaningful exposure to French in order to develop a native-like accent when speaking. It took Natsuko one year of attending school full-time. How long would it take you to reach 2,000 hours of listening?

- 15 min per day: 21.9 years

- 30 min per day: 10.95 years

- 45 min per day: 7.3 years

- 60 min per day: 5.48 years

- 90 min (the length of a movie) per day: 3.65 years

Now, does this mean you need to spend 2,000 hours listening to French before you can start speaking? Not at all. You will be able to have a perfectly enjoyable conversation in French well before that. It is also not necessary for you to have a native-like accent in French, like Natsuko had in English - you certainly do not. However, if you do have ambitions to speak natural French it is helpful to have a sense of perspective about how long it might take, and a real-life example to contemplate. The main lesson I took from watching Natsuko's English transform over the course of a year was this: You must spend a lot of time listening to your new language.

Luckily, you can slash this figure of 2,000 hours by bringing to the table something that an eight-year-old child cannot: study skills. A child may be sponge-like in their ability to pick up new sounds, and have a wonderful lack of inhibition that allows them to embrace any learning opportunity, but as an adult, you can grasp learning opportunities on an intellectual level that can allow you to learn far faster.

Tips for Improving Your Accent

The first step in developing a good French accent is to learn to listen to and notice the rhythm and melody of a French accent. Listening comes before speaking. If you cannot hear it, you cannot say it. Here are some practical steps to follow to develop a good French accent:

1. Listen closely to native French speakers' pronunciation of interesting words and phrases. Replay them in your mind and repeat them to yourself aloud.

2. Record yourself saying these words and phrases, and listen back. (The phone in your pocket is great for this. Look for the voice recorder app.) You will probably be surprised at the difference between how you think you sound and how you sound in reality.

3. If you have a French friend or teacher, ask them to record the same vocabulary and send them to you in a voice message. Pay close attention to the differences, and copy them yourself.

4. Try hard to copy the rhythm and melody of the phrases you learn. Listen to them over and over and see if any melodies or rhythms emerge. Try to involve the other senses in your learning (clapping, humming, singing, etc.).

5. Learn songs. Singers articulate the lyrics of songs clearly in order to make themselves understood, so songs are an excellent resource for accent and

pronunciation. The effort involved in memorising lyrics in French and the mental processing involved in associating words with melodies means that you will pay very close attention to the sounds of the words. In the process, your pronunciation will improve quickly. This does take longer, but comes with great rewards!

Olly's Tip:

When working on your accent, practise saying aloud complete phrases rather than single words. Not only does the way you say a word change when you put it in a sentence, but practising complete phrases will help you become confident speaking in longer, flowing sentences. If you feel silly putting on a French accent when saying complete sentences aloud, that is a good sign! Usually, the sillier you think you sound, the more progress you are making, as you are breaking your ties with English!

Part 3: Mastering French Vocabulary - How to Memorise Any French Word You Need

Chapter 11 - Taking Advantage of What You Already Know

When learning French as a beginner, one of your most important jobs is to grow your vocabulary. There is simply no escaping the fact that you have to learn a large number of new words in order to speak a foreign language. Of course, grammar is also important, but enlarging your vocabulary is the fastest way to improve your ability to express yourself effectively in French.

Think of it this way: With lots of grammar and no vocabulary, you cannot express anything. However, with lots of vocabulary and no grammar, you can express a lot. What this means is if you spend all your time learning French grammar rules, but you do not know enough words, you will not be able to speak. On the other hand, if you focus on growing a large vocabulary, you will probably be able to make yourself understood in most situations, even if your grammar leaves something to be desired.

Although reaching a high level of proficiency in French requires you to know several thousand words, you can do a lot as a beginner with just a small vocabulary. An important language learning strategy, then, as a beginner, is not to learn every single word you come across, but rather to focus on learning important vocabulary you can use to communicate right away - but more on this later.

The first question is: How should you go about learning all the words you need to know to start speaking French? Different languages have different challenges but, as we have already seen, the one advantage English speakers have learning French is that the two languages share a lot of common vocabulary. These are words you already know in English that are the same (or very similar) in French, and these mutually-intelligible words are known as *cognates*. The greatest number of these have come to English from French over the last 1,000 years, and a few common examples are:

[11.1]

- révolution - revolution
- théâtre - theatre
- géographie - geography

As you can see, apart from the addition of an accent or two, or a slightly different spelling, these words are almost identical. In addition, more recently, French has begun to borrow words rather extensively from English, and many English words are now in daily use in the French language, for example *sandwich, weekend, hamburger, hot dog, football*. Other words have been absorbed into French and have taken on new (and sometimes slightly bizarre) meanings:

[11.2]

- baskets - trainers, running shoes (from the idea of "basketball shoes" or sneakers)

- hand - handball (shortened form, the word "handball" is also used)

- foot – football (shortened form of "football", the same as for "handball")

This shared vocabulary makes French much easier to learn than languages like Chinese or Vietnamese since there are far more cognates (incidentally, Vietnamese does have quite a few words that come from French due to the French colonisation of the country - but that is another story!). It even makes French easier to learn than other closely related languages like German or Italian since the number of words shared by English and French is so high.

Another factor that will help you as a new learner of French is that there are groups of words that follow more or less predictable patterns, so if a word ends in a particular way in English, there is a good chance that it will have a corresponding ending in French.

Here are some common patterns to remember:

[11.3 - 11.6]

-ty becomes -té

- personality - personnalité

- society - société
- equality - égalité

-ly becomes -ement

- finally - finalement
- particularly - particulièrement
- temporarily - temporairement
- currently - actuellement

-tion stays -tion

- ambition - ambition
- coalition - coalition
- cessation - cessation

-ssion becomes -ssion

- recession - récession (economic)
- oppression - oppression
- admission - admission

You can find even more examples of common French cognates in Appendix 2 at the end of this book.

You may have heard of so-called *false friends*. False friends are words that may look similar, and may have come from the same root, but have since developed different meanings in French and English. For example, *actuellemtent* means "at the moment, presently" and *éventuellement* means "possibly, potentially". In Appendix 3 is an extensive list of false friends to watch out for.

However, false friends are relatively few and far between, and the result is that you start out with a large bulk of "free" vocabulary that does not need to be learnt. If you do not know a word, you can often just try to guess and you will find that more often than not, it works!

Chapter 12 - Choosing the Right Vocabulary

The French language is estimated to have around 100,000 words, but you already know that you do not need all these words in order to communicate. The lesson to draw from this high number is that every language has far more words than you could ever possibly learn or would ever need to use. To begin with, then, it is important to accept that you cannot learn every French word you ever meet, and nor should you.

Imagine you are trying to read *Vingt mille lieues sous les mers* (Twenty Thousand Leagues Under the Sea) by Jules Vernes - in the original French. It was published in 1870 and includes a lot of vocabulary relevant to nineteenth century seafaring and navigation. How useful do you think this vocabulary is going to be to you in the twenty-first century? It is safe to say you do not need to try to remember it all. Imagine you did try to look all the words up in a dictionary, write them down and remember them. You would spend a lot of time learning words you are never likely to need, get bogged down and reading the book would become a chore.

You may think this is an extreme example, but not so! If you take a look through a random selection of French language courses on the market today, many will set their dialogues and lessons in outdated or impractical situations. Classic examples would be changing travellers' cheques or booking hotel rooms over the phone - two things that have been made all but obsolete by the internet. Consequently, not only is this vocabulary not useful to you, but you would spend time learning it at the expense of other vocabulary that you would be far more likely to use, such as asking for the Wi-Fi password!

Once you become comfortable with the idea that you do not need to learn every new word you encounter, this can free you up to ask a different question: *"What vocabulary should I learn?"* Part of learning French quickly involves training yourself to take an active role in choosing what to learn - vocabulary that will be useful in your life and is relevant to your goals - and focusing on that vocabulary. Identifying which vocabulary will be most useful to you comes with practice. For now, the easiest approach is to identify which words in your textbook you are *not* likely to need, and to be comfortable skipping them. If any given particular word turns out to be important after all, you can be sure it will come up again!

In the following sections we will look at techniques and devices for learning new French words and the gender of those words.

Chapter 13 - Remembering the Gender of French Words

In Chapter 4, I introduced the concept of word gender and the fact that French nouns are either masculine or feminine. When you learn a French noun, an inherent part of the identity of that noun is whether it is masculine (*le*) or feminine (*la*). Right from the beginning of your French study, you must make sure to learn the gender of each word you learn. Do not be tempted to skip this and say: "*I will learn the gender later!*", as this kind of bad habit can be impossible to correct down the road. If you get into the habit of associating each word with a gender from the beginning, you will find it quickly becomes easier to do, and you will develop tricks to help yourself remember. The first few are always the hardest!

Many people find it helpful to use imagery to remember the gender of nouns. Try this:

> *Whenever you meet a new noun, try to create an image, word association or "hook" that nods to the gender of the word, and build into the way you remember the word.*

For example, if you wanted to remember that the French word for table - *la table* - is feminine, you might picture a particularly feminine-looking table, and use that as your "hook". Perhaps this imaginary table is a small toy table that lives inside an extravagantly feminine doll's house that would make it impossible for you to think of a masculine **le table*. (Note: stereotypes are your friend when creating visual associations!)

The French word for planet - *la planète* - is also feminine. Knowing this, you could visualise a newly-discovered planet in our solar system. The planet in your mind could be a bright, vibrant feminine colour, inhabited by a population of only women. Thinking of **le planète* in the future would not be hard!

If you are a particularly visual learner, you might use different colours for each gender when you write in your notebook or create flashcards. For example, you could use green cards for masculine nouns and red cards for feminine nouns. How you do this is up to you, but try to leave mental breadcrumbs for yourself as you learn each new word. By building this technique into your learning when you start, it will help you in the long run.

Chapter 14 - Making Words Stick: How to Memorize French Vocabulary

In the previous chapter, we learnt a technique for remembering the gender of words, so that you do not feel overwhelmed with the prospect of learning an additional piece of information (the gender) along with each new item of vocabulary. Now that you know how to approach learning the gender of words, let's discuss how to approach learning the words themselves.

As any person becomes experienced at language learning, they gradually begin to discover which techniques work well for them. When it comes to learning vocabulary, there exists a vast array of so-called "memory techniques", ranging from the dull to the eccentric. In this chapter, I will describe a way to approach learning new vocabulary I have developed that draws on best practice from the world of language learning and memory improvement.

It is called the A.R.T. Technique, which stands for:

- Attention

- Repetition

- Try

The A.R.T. Technique is not a prescriptive memory technique. Rather, it represents three different phases of learning a new word, from the first time you encounter it all the way through to truly "knowing" that word. Encoding these steps in a process not only helps you to structure your learning, but, more importantly, helps you to identify steps you might be missing which represent an opportunity for improvement. Think of it as the *A.R.T. of Memory*!

The A.R.T. Technique

The A.R.T. Technique basically assumes that every new word you learn needs to go through a certain number of steps before it lodges itself in your long-term bank of usable vocabulary that belongs to you - that you *own*.

Attention

The first part of the journey is A which stands for "Attention": you need to notice the word, to become familiar with it, to put it in your mouth and chew it to see what it tastes like. It is no good just to see a French word and connect it to an English translation, you need a hook to hang it on in your memory. There are various ways of doing this. Maybe the word is very similar-sounding to an English word. An example would be *un bol*, "a bowl". In this case, it is very easy to remember.

Other words might not be immediately obvious but may still lead you to think of a word in English. For example, the French word *queue* primarily means "tail" but most English speakers would recognise it from the English word "queue" as in "stand in line". In fact, the French expression *faire la queue*, which literally means "make the tail", is one way to say "queue up" in French. These two different meanings reinforce each other and it suddenly becomes easy to remember both.

In less clear cases, you can associate words with something in English that helps you remember them, albeit in a roundabout way! For example, *porter* means "to carry" which is easy to remember because in a hotel, a porter "carries" your bags. In this case, there is a real association since the words come from the same root.

Some French words may have no connection with English whatsoever, but if you are creative enough, you can usually manufacture an association in your mind. For example, you might remember *pain* is French for "bread" because "bread is a pain to make". It does not matter how creative, ridiculous or far-fetched a word association sounds - as long as your "hook" helps you remember a new word, you have taken it one step closer to entering your long-term memory.

Olly's Tip:

When it comes to creating word associations students often complain they lack the creativity. In my experience, everyone is creative, they simply need a bit of practice at it! The important thing to realise about this activity is that the longer you take to invent a image, the stronger the association will be, so you should not worry if it takes time at the start - it will speed up! When I am learning new vocabulary in a difficult language, I will sometimes sit for as long as 5-10 minutes with one word, thinking about possible associations and "hooks".

> *I find this to be a good use of time, because once the penny drops the imagery I have created will usually last a long time and I will never worry about forgetting the word again! Remember, as we saw in* Chapter 12, *you should be selective about the vocabulary you choose to learn - you do not need to use this process for every word in French!*

To provide you with as much inspiration as possible for the "Attention" part of the technique, let's look at some more examples.

Some words may be best remembered in groups. *Une chaussure* is "a shoe", *une chaussette* is "a sock" and *un chausson* is "a slipper". The three words go together, you get a feel for them, and suddenly they become easy to remember because of their similarities.

The French word *un roman* is "a novel". You might remember this by imagining a roman soldier sitting on his chair on guard duty engrossed in a good book.

You might try to make up word games like this: the French word *ou* means "or" but the word *où* (with an accent) means "where". They are both pronounced the same but when you write them, how can you remember which one needs an accent? Ask yourself the question, *where* is the accent? The answer is: the accent is on "*where*" - easy!

Some words might be easily remembered because you have encountered them elsewhere, such as in French expressions. For example, you might remember *dieu* means "God" because you have heard French people saying *mon dieu!* That is French for "Oh my God!"

Finally, you might remember words just because they are funny. You ride the *métro* in Paris and you notice that those fold up chairs you get on trains are called *strapontins*. It looks like "strap on tins" - what a funny thing to call them! However, it is certainly memorable and you probably will not forget *strapontins* after that even though it is quite an obscure word.

The examples given above all demonstrate how to give your full "Attention" to the word you are learning - the first stage in the process. Take your time and explore the word, looking at it from as many different angles as possible. This may seem difficult at first but with practice you will soon get used to the process, and quite possibly addicted, once you see the powerful effect it has on your memory. If one particular word is causing you stress, leave it alone and walk away. If that word is important, you will see it again. Relax and enjoy the process of creating associations!

Learning Words in Context

In Chapter 9 we looked at homophones - words that can have different meanings in different contexts. Take the English verb "get", for example. This word has so many different meanings, for example "get on a bus", "get drunk", "get a present for your birthday", "get given something" and so on, and if you told someone studying English to learn the word "get", it would be an impossible task. So, how should you approach memorising French homophones with the A.R.T. Technique? Remember that this is more of a theoretical concern than a practical one - when you hear the word in a different context you will notice immediately that something is different. When it comes to learning a homophone yourself, the best advice is to learn the word in the context in which you meet it and learn other meanings later when you come to them. This means you can stick to the doctrine of learning what is useful to you and not waste your time learning extra information that you do not need.

Note also that very often there is no direct translation between English and French. In English, for example, we have the word "river" but French distinguishes between *rivière* and *fleuve*. A *fleuve* is the big river that all the other tributary rivers flow into and that flows into the sea - so the River Thames and the Seine in French are considered *fleuves* and not *rivières*. In English, we have no equivalent word and you just need to learn the French word as it is without connecting it to an English word.

There are many ways you can create a "hook" for a word, and here I have offered just a few examples. You will find you start to come up with new and inventive ways to dig your teeth into a word, to become familiar with it and to know its personality. This is the first step of the A.R.T. Technique - Attention.

Repetition

Next comes R, which stands for "Repetition", something that is key to the development of any skill and language learning is no exception. Think of learning to play the piano or how to play tennis; you repeat the same piece of music or practise the same strokes over and over, improving a little each time, until it becomes automatic. When a baby learns her first language, all she does for years is repeat what she hears around her, gradually refining what she says as new words are introduced and she observes her parents' reactions. For the baby, endless repetition results in learning. However, as an adult, you are unlikely to be surrounded by native French speakers who can help you practise all day long. As such, you need to be more intentional about practising your new vocabulary. Being systematic about the repetition of vocabulary requires a plan.

When you meet a new French word, you are unlikely to remember it first time; you might need to see the new word five or ten times before it sticks. You may find this forgetfulness frustrating at first, but when you understand that forgetting a new word is normal, you can then begin to figure out how to address the problem. The "Forgetting Curve" is a concept commonly seen in discussions of memory. What the "Forgetting Curve" essentially shows is that your memory is strengthened by repeat exposure to a piece of information. The very first time you learn something new, you might forget it quickly. When you are reminded of that information a second time, you will retain it for a bit longer. The third time you see that information, it will take even longer to forget, and so on. The lesson for us as language learners is that we must plan to see a new item of vocabulary multiple times, remembering it for a little longer each time, if we intend to remember it for the long-term. This is where your brain needs a little bit of help.

Since you are not guaranteed to meet a new French word again after you first learn it, you need to come up with a way that ensures you will see the word again at regular intervals, if you want to be sure to learn it. Among the many ways of creating repetition for foreign language vocabulary, the most popular method is to use flashcards. With flashcards, you can regularly and systematically recycle your new vocabulary items until they are fixed in your long-term memory. Blank index cards can be bought online or in any stationary shop, on to which you can simply write your new word in French on one side and the translation on the other.

If you own a computer, smartphone or tablet, you can also use digital flashcard apps to organise your learning. Using electronic flashcards is my preferred method for learning vocabulary, because not only can you store all your new vocabulary in one place, but the built-in algorithm of the software can automatically space out the repetition of your words at smart intervals that optimise your learning. By indicating to the app how well you know a particular word (easy, medium, hard), the algorithm knows which words you find easy and will recycle them less frequently. Conversely, the vocabulary you struggle with you will see more often.

Olly's Tip:

Remember once again what we said earlier about learning words that are most useful to you. Flashcards can quickly become overwhelming if you attempt to create a card for every word under the sun. By focusing on only learning words that you perceive to be immediately useful to you, you can make the process of repetition more efficient and less of a chore.

Bonus Resource: If you would like to learn more about my method of using electronic flashcards to learn vocabulary quickly, you might enjoy my guide Make Words Stick, available here: http://iwillteachyoualanguage.com/makewordsstick

Try

If you have followed the procedure described in the A.R.T. Technique so far, you will have:

- Brought your full Attention to the new word, creating a hook to help you remember the meaning

- Planned for Repetition of the new word, so you can minimise your chances of forgetting it

This brings us, finally, to T, the final ingredient in the technique. The T in A.R.T. stands for "Try". This is the final step in the process of learning a word that gives you full ownership of that word, so you can not only understand it, but can recall and use the word freely in conversation. It is often here that self-study language courses reach the limits of their utility. A self-study course may offer you plenty of language *input* - new words and phrases - and even exercises to help with learning and repetition, but there is no opportunity for *output* - using what you have learnt in meaningful conversation. You see, learning the meaning of a new word or understanding the word when it is spoken, is not enough by itself. It is only when you actually try to use a new word in conversation - the feeling of physically saying the word and seeing if it produces the desired effect in the discussion - that you can begin to say that you truly know a word.

Perhaps we could take our earlier tennis analogy a little further and imagine that if you do A(ttention) and R(epetition) without T(ry), it is a bit like taking tennis lessons with a coach, practising the shots, but never actually playing against a human opponent. The reason you learn tennis is to play against other people and it is only through competing in a match that you can really understand the game and improve. You cannot say you are a good tennis player if you never play against someone, nor can you say you are able to speak a language if you never open your mouth.

This could even be rule number one for language learners - use what you know. Even if you only know how to say "hello", then take every opportunity to say it, and say it with confidence. As you learn more expressions, seek out situations where you can experiment. You will inevitably make mistakes but it is this experimentation that fine-tunes the language you have learnt and fixes it in your memory. In a tennis match, you try a shot that does not come off, but you notice what you did wrong, and next time you play the shot differently. With language learning the process is identical: you try out a new word in a sentence and notice it may not be quite right; you make a slight adjustment next time and try again. This is how you build your vocabulary and gain confidence in your language ability.

Just remember, this last part - the T in A.R.T. - is what it is all about! Speaking with people and Trying out your new vocabulary is why you learn a language in the first place, so do remember to enjoy yourself and not be put off by mistakes.

What Have We Learnt About Memorising Vocabulary?

Let's review...

- Growing your vocabulary is a fundamental part of learning French, and without vocabulary you can say nothing.

- English speakers learning French have the advantage of vocabulary with shared roots (cognates).

- Despite finding cognates relatively easy to learn, you will still face a large number of unfamiliar French words which you will need to learn and place into your long-term memory

- When choosing words to learn, prioritise vocabulary that is relevant to you and that you are likely to need - *"It is in my textbook!"* is not a good reason.

- Try not to get frustrated when you forget a new word, as it is an inevitable part of learning.

The A.R.T. Technique:

- Every word you learn will pass through a number of stages. Sometimes, this happens naturally. Other times, you need to be more deliberate about the learning process.

- First comes A, "attention". Get to know the word, chew it, swill it round your mouth like wine, become familiar with it and find a way to hook it into your memory.

- Next comes R, "repetition". Constant repetition and reviewing will help fix it into your memory. You cannot remember every word first time, but after seeing it a number of times, it will begin stick. Make the review of vocabulary a part of your language routine, using a system such as flashcards.

- Finally, T, "try". You only truly know a word once you have used it in conversation with a real person. This is why you are learning French in the first place!

You will experience a feeling of success and achievement when you begin to have your first conversations in French using words and phrases you have learnt. Having conversations, albeit simple ones, and beginning to communicate in French will only reinforce your desire to continue to improve. Having spent this chapter exploring vocabulary, we will now move on to discuss learning French grammar.

Part 4: Tackling French Grammar

Chapter 15 - Nouns, Adjectives & Gender

Making Sense of French Nouns

Let's start from the very beginning. What exactly is a noun? A noun is a word used to identify people, places, or things. For example, "dog", "chief, "town" and "flower" are all nouns. In addition to physical objects, the following are also nouns: "love", "hunger" and "wisdom" - these are known as *abstract nouns* because they describe an idea or quality, rather than a physical object. It is interesting to note that the French word for "noun", *nom*, also means "name".

In French, all nouns have a gender, either *masculine* or *feminine*. When a noun represents something with an obvious gender, such as "boy", the grammatical gender will be exactly what you expect:

[15.1]

- "a boy" is un garçon (masculine)

- "a girl" is une fille (feminine).

However, other kinds of objects may not follow any logical pattern. For example, while buses and wine are masculine:

[15.2]

- un autobus
- un vin

...cars and beer are feminine:

[15.3]

- une voiture
- une bière

Sometimes the gender of a noun can be counterintuitive - for example, "masculinity" (*la masculinité*), and "virility" (*la virilité*) are both feminine nouns in French!

As we have already seen, learning the gender of nouns is an important habit, but a habit which gets easier over time, and advice for learning noun genders can be found in Chapter 13. It is also essential to remember that making an error with the gender of a noun in conversation does not usually matter one bit! For example, if you are in a bar and you order *un bière*, instead of *une bière*, there is no chance of the barman giving you the wrong drink.

While there are no steadfast rules for guessing the gender of nouns, there are nevertheless some guidelines that will help you, and will be correct *most* of the time. These guidelines are based on word endings, and while not infallible, will help you make a good guess at the noun gender.

[15.4 - 15.9]

Masculine

- Words Ending -on
    - un poisson - a fish (exception: une chanson, a song)
- Words Ending -eur
    - un ordinateur - a computer (exception: la chaleur, the heat)
- Words Ending -eau
    - le niveau - the level (exception: la peau, the skin)
- Words Ending -isme, -asme
    - le communisme - communism
- Words Ending -ède, -ège, -ème
    - un piège - a trap (exception: la crème, cream)
- Words Ending -age
    - un message - a message (exception: une cage)

Most words borrowed from English are masculine (*le weekend*, the weekend, exception: *une interview*, an interview) and countries, rivers, fruit and vegetables <u>not ending</u> in -e are masculine (*le Vietnam*, Vietnam, *un melon*, a melon).

[15.10 - 15.13]

Feminine

- Words Ending -te, -tié
    - la beauté - beauty (exception: pâté, pâté)
- Words Ending -ée
    - une année - a year (exception: un musée, a museum)
- Words Ending -elle
    - une coccinelle - a ladybird
- Words Ending -te, -tte, -ette
    - la date - the date (exception: un squelette, a skeleton)
- Nouns with any of the following endings are almost always feminine:
    - -aison
    - -ssion
    - -tion
    - -xion

Many abstract nouns are feminine whatever their ending, and countries, rivers, fruit and vegetables ending in -e are usually feminine (*La France*, France; *une pomme*, an apple;

exceptions: *le Cambodge*, Cambodia; *un légume*, a vegetable).

The guidelines above are not exhaustive, nor is the list of exceptions, but it gives an example of the kind of thing you can look to for help when you need to guess the gender of a noun. I do not suggest you try to commit this list of word endings to memory. Instead, read through the list a few times in order to raise your awareness of the word endings and gender patterns, and then do your best to notice these patterns in new vocabulary you find as you read and listen to French.

For some French words, these shortcuts do not apply, and the only solution is to remember the gender through practice and repetition, and using the techniques described in Chapter 13. You will find that the gender of the most common French words soon becomes second nature, simply because you will encounter these words so often. You will quickly learn that a bank is *une banque* (feminine) and that a bed is *un lit* (masculine) and before long it sounds very unnatural to say **un banque* or **une lit*. This instinctive feeling of what is correct or incorrect is how native speakers know the gender of their nouns - it simply *is*. French people do not spend hours learning noun genders, it just sounds wrong to them - similar to the way an English speaker would never say "I goes". This is how it should be for learners of French, too, and the key to achieving this is to get as much exposure as possible to the French language through listening and reading. As your exposure to French increases, so you will develop an instinctive knowledge of the gender of words.

Articles - What They Are and How to Use Them

An "article" is small grammatical word we use to introduce a noun. In English, the articles are:

- a

- the

In French, the articles change slightly depending on the gender of the noun. The masculine articles are:

[15.14]

- un - a/an

- le - the

The French feminine articles are:

[15.15]

- une - a/an

- la - the

Just like in English, the article comes just before the noun, for example:

[15.16]

- un œuf - an egg (masculine)

- une robe - a dress (feminine)

- le monde - the world (masculine)

- la bière - the beer (feminine)

You already know the importance of learning the gender of French words, and so when you review your new vocabulary it is important to always include the article along with the word - "*le* monde", not just "monde". It is good practice to say new words aloud, not in your head or whispering under your breath, but speaking them in a full, clear voice. Speaking the words aloud, along with the correct masculine or feminine article, will help you get used to the sound of the article and the word together, which strengthens your memory. Eventually, it will become as unthinkable for you to say *un banque* as it would be for a French person, partly because it simply sounds wrong!

Note that when the definite article comes before a word that begins with a vowel, they are combined. For example, "the egg" would be *l'œuf*, not *le œuf*. French also uses a plural article – *les*. The same plural article is used for both masculine and feminine plurals:

- les enfants

- les robes

It is also important to be aware that there is a unique type of article in French which we do not have in English: the partitive article. The French partitive articles are:

- du (masculine singular)

- de la (feminine singular)

- d' (masculine or feminine in front of a vowel)

- des (plural)

The partitive articles in French correspond to "some" or "any" in English. However, in English we normally just omit these words.

- J'ai mangé de la salade hier – I ate (some) salad yesterday.

- Est-ce que vous avez des questions ? – Do you have (any) questions ?

- Je bois du café – I drink (some) coffee

Olly's Tip:

Saying the article along with the noun can seem unnecessary for English speakers, because the article never changes in English - we only have "the" and "a". In French, though, the article is more important because it tells you the gender of the word. Try to get into the habit of including the "le" or "la", "un" or "une" in your practice from the beginning - it will make things much easier later on!

How to Describe Things: Adjectives in French

We saw in the last section how the gender of a noun determines the article you use; since "banque" is feminine, you must say "*la* banque". However, the importance of gender does not stop at choosing the correct article. The gender of the noun will also affect another important word class: the adjective.

An adjective is a word that describes a noun, such as "intelligent" in "the intelligent man". In English, the adjective never changes its form. In French, however, the adjective must *agree with* the noun. When we say an adjective must *agree with* a noun, it means that the adjective will change slightly depending on whether the noun is masculine or feminine. The masculine form of the adjective goes with a masculine word, and the feminine form of the adjective goes with a feminine word.

An example will help to clarify. In French, the word for "intelligent" is *intelligent* but the feminine form adds an "e" and becomes *intelligente*. As such, "an intelligent man" would be:

[15.17]

- un homme intelligent

But an intelligent woman would be:

- une femme intelligente

As you can see, the masculine form, *intelligent*, changes to *intelligente* to agree with *femme*, "woman".

Depending on the ending, adjectives change in different ways. Here are some common examples:

[15.18 - 15.22]

- Words Ending -e remain the same
    - rouge (m.), rouge (f.) - red
- Words Ending -ier
    - dernier (m.), dernière (f.) – last
- Words Ending -c*
    - public (m.), publique (f.) - public
    - blanc (m.), blanche (f.) - white
    - sec (m.), sèche (f.) - dry
- Words Ending -f
    - pensif (m.) pensive (f.) - thoughtful, pensive
    - bref (m.), brève (f.) - brief, short
- Words Ending -x
    - heureux (m.), heureuse (f.) - happy
    - doux (m.), douce (f.) - soft

*There are several other possibilities for adjectives ending in "c" than those shown here.

One final point to note is that words ending in -e remain the same in both the masculine and feminine forms. Since lots of words in French end in -e, this simplifies things for you considerably. Again, this list of adjective endings is not exhaustive, but it will help you to start to notice certain patterns among the word endings, patterns which will soon become familiar and intuitive to you.

Olly's Tip:

Do not be put off if adjective-noun agreement seems complicated. So often, things only seem difficult because they are unfamiliar. At this stage, try to simply notice how the grammar behaves - you do not need to memorise any word endings. You will be astonished at how quickly you get used to French grammar once you spend more time listening and reading to the language. Patience is a virtue in language learning!

Chapter 16 - Verb Conjugations Made Easy

In addition to noun gender, the other thing you probably remember from learning French at school is memorising tables of verbs. Let's begin with a definition. What is a verb? A verb is a word that describes action, otherwise known as a "doing words". Examples of verbs would be: "hit", "study" and "go".

In English, verb forms sometimes change according to who does the action. In the present tense, we add an "s" to the he/she/it (3rd person) form of the verb:

- I wait

- You wait

- He/she/it waits

Verbs also change depending on when the action happens:

- I begin

- I began

- I have begun

French verbs are similar, but French verbs change slightly more than in English:

[16.1]

- je mange - i eat

- tu manges* - you eat

- il/elle mange - he/she eats

- nous mangeons - we eat

- vous mangez* - you eat

- ils mangent - they eat

*In French, there is more than one way to say "you". The *tu* form is used when talking to someone you know well and are on friendly terms with. However, there is also the *vous* form, which is used when speaking to:

- more than one person

- someone you do not know

- someone to whom you need to show respect

In French, there are three types of verbs which are *regular* and follow predictable patterns. Regular verbs belong to one of three groups ("conjugations") and they end in either -er, -re, or -ir. Here is what they look like in the present tense:

[16.2 - 16.4]

-er (1st conjugation)

Parler - to speak

- je parle - i speak
- tu parles - you speak
- il/elle parle - he/she speaks
- nous parlons - we speak
- vous parlez - you speak
- ils/elles parlent - they speak

-re (2nd conjugation)

Vendre - to sell

- je vends - i sell
- tu vends - you sell
- il/elle vend - he/she sells
- nous vendons - we sell
- vous vendez - you sell
- ils/elles vendent - they sell

-ir (3rd conjugation)

Finir - to finish

- je finis - i finish
- tu finis - you finish
- il/elle finit - he/she finishes
- nous finissons - we finish
- vous finissez - you finish
- ils/elles finissent - they finish

The first point to note is that for all three conjugations, although the "I", "you" and "he/she" forms may be spelled differently, the pronunciation is identical (so *parle* and *parles* are pronounced the same with no "s" sound, while *finis* and *finit* are both pronounced the same with no "s" or "t" sound) which makes spoken French much easier than it might first seem. You will also notice that for all three conjugations, the plural (*nous*, *vous* and *ils/elles*) endings are the same across the three conjugations and it is simply the base ("stem") that changes, so in fact there is really nothing too complicated to remember.

The second point to bear in mind is that while verb conjugations need to be learnt by heart, this is no more difficult than learning to count or say the alphabet, and simply by repeating them out loud several times over a period of days, you will soon remember them and be able to use them without thinking - in the same way that always repeating the article with a noun when you say it helps you remember the gender quickly and naturally.

As with most languages, there are also *irregular* verbs - verbs which do not follow the standard patterns. Irregular verbs do not obey the rules and must be learnt by heart individually. Many irregular verbs are some of the most common verbs in French, words like *aller*, "to go" or *vouloir*, "to want", and at first, this might appear to be bad news since you are required to learn lots of irregular verbs before you can begin to express even simple ideas. In practice, however, the opposite is true. Since many of these irregular verbs are so common, you will see them frequently right from the start which means you will quickly become accustomed to their forms and you will know instinctively to say *je vais* or *tu vas* ("I go", "you go") without having to think about it. Focus on mastering the first-person forms (I go, I want, etc.) first as these are the ones you will use most often. Here is the present tense of these two verbs as an example:

[16.5 - 16.6]

Aller - to go

- je vais - i go
- tu vas - you go
- il/elle va - he/she goes
- nous allons - we go
- vouz allez - you go
- ils/elles vont - they go

Vouloir - to want

- je veux - i want
- tu veux - you want
- il/elle veut - he/she wants
- nous voulons - we want
- vous voulez - you want
- ils/elles veulent - they want

There is nothing terribly difficult about verb conjugations in French, especially once you become more familiar with the language. Having said that, verb conjugations still need to be learnt and memorised. So, what is the best way to do this? The ultimate goal is for these words to be fixed in your long term-memory and to become so familiar that you produce the correct form without thinking, much the same as when you say "I go" or "she goes" in English. The best way to do this is through a combination of techniques.

How to Remember French Verb Conjugations

In language learning, memorising lists is rarely a good thing, but in the case of verb conjugations, a certain amount of repetition will get you off to a good start. You will assimilate verb conjugations naturally by using them and practising, but repeating the tables early on can act like stabilisers on the bicycle before you can ride by yourself. Do not try to learn too much at once - start with the present tense of the three regular conjugations given above, and repeat them until you know them by heart and without hesitation. It will help to try both reciting the verb tables out loud and also writing them down from memory; the combination of the two approaches together will help to cement them in your memory.

If you practise the basic verb conjugations for ten or fifteen minutes every day, it will only take a few days to completely master the regular verbs in the present tense. Once you feel confident with these, you can start working on some of the new irregular verbs you meet as you study. Repeat the same process and you will soon find you can remember many of them with ease. Later, when you meet other tenses or other verb forms, you can once again use the same techniques.

Learning verb tables is only a crutch for you to lean on at the beginning, however. The way you will master verbs is the same way as learning a new word - through usage ("Try"). Once you know the verbs and start to use them in different contexts, they will hook themselves into your long-term memory and, providing you do not entirely stop speaking French, will stay there for a long time.

Olly's Tip:

I am not a fan of rote memorisation in language learning. However, there are some cases in which a bit of hard work and rote learning at the beginning can quickly pay off, by getting you past a hurdle which could otherwise hold you back. Learning the alphabet of an unfamiliar language (such as Japanese or Arabic) is one example of where rote learning helps. Memorising basic verb conjugations is another.

If you focus, you can have the basic -ar, -re and -ir verb conjugations memorised within a few days at most. Once memorised, you can get on with the rest of your French study, which is far more enjoyable! To aid you in the process of learning irregular verbs, it can help to get a good workbook with dedicated practice exercises. Visit http://www.iwillteachyoualanguage.com/resources *for a full list of recommendations.*

French Verbs - Spelling and Pronunciation

Just as with other French words, not all of the letters written in verbs are pronounced. You may have noticed this if you listened to the audio recording of the verbs given above. For example:

- The "s" in *manges* is silent and is pronounced exactly the same as *mange*

- With *vends* and *vend*, the "ds" and "d" are not pronounced so both words are pronounced as "von" with the nasal "n" that we saw in the pronunciation section

- In *finis* and *finit*, the "s" and the "t" are both silent, meaning they are both pronounced "fini"

- Lastly, the -ent at the end of the *ils/elles* ("they") forms is silent. This is true for every verb in French - the "nt" is never pronounced and is completely silent.

As ever, the best way to learn the pronunciation of these verb endings is to simply pay close attention to the audio recordings as you learn your verb tables. Imitate what you hear and try not to let the spelling mislead you! Once you are aware of the silent letters in verbs, you will begin to recognise them easily and they will be become part of the characteristics of the verbs you learn.

Chapter 17 - Putting Sentences Together: Word Order

In simple sentences, French word order is more or less the same as in English which follows a structure known as *subject-verb-object*. For example:

[17.1]

- la fille lit le livre - the girl (subject) reads (verb) the book (object)

The first difference comes when we add an adjective to the sentence, since adjectives usually follow the noun they describe:

[17.2]

- la fille lit le livre rouge - the girl reads the red book

Some adjectives usually come before the noun, *la jolie fille*, the "pretty girl" and yet others have different meanings depending on whether they are placed before the noun or after. For example, the word *propre* before a noun means "own" (as in "my own"), whereas after the noun it means "clean". As such:

- ma propre chemise - my own shirt

- ma chemise propre - my clean shirt

You can even have *ma propre chemise propre* which would mean "my own clean shirt"!

Things start to get a little more involved when we throw words like "me", "you", "him", "it" (object pronouns) into the mix, because in French these words go *before* the verb instead of *after* as in English. For example:

- je vois David - I see David

- je le vois - I see him

In the above example, can you see how *David* not only changes to *le* ("him"]), but also moves its position in the sentence?

Sometimes, other pronouns might be thrown into the sentence if there is more than one person or thing involved. Take the sentence "I give the book to David". In this sentence, we can replace both "the book" and "to David" with pronouns, which we might do in order to avoid repetition, giving us a sentence like: "I give it to him". Here is how we arrive at this sentence in French:

- je donne - I give

- je le donne - I give it

- je le lui donne - I give it to him

In the above example, *le* means "it" and *lui* means "to him". What is more interesting than a technical explanation at this point is to simply point out that a lot of information can come

121

before the verb in French, whereas in English the information would come after the verb.

When it comes to asking questions in French there are some similarities with English. In English, it is possible to make a question just using the intonation of your voice, so "you have a girlfriend" (statement) becomes "you have a girlfriend?" (question) just by raising the tone of your voice. This way of asking a question is even more common in French than in English, and is probably the most colloquial way of asking a question: *Tu as une copine?* You might even notice that French people often tend to use this device when speaking English rather more than native English speakers!

Another way to form a question in French is to invert the verb and the subject, giving:

[17.3]

- voulez-vous... ? - do you want...? (lit: want you)

- pensez-vous...? - do you think...? (lit: think you)

A third way to form a question is to add *est-ce que* to the beginning of a statement, so *vous voulez un café*, "you want a coffee" (statement) becomes:

[17.4]

- Est-ce que vous voulez un café? - Do you want a coffee? (question)

Olly's Tip:

Est-ce que is one of the most useful ways to ask a question, but do not worry about the meaning of the words est-ce que *right now. It looks like a fiddly phrase, but its function is extremely simple - just remember it as a little phrase you can attach to any statement to turn it into a question.*

With language learning more broadly, it is often tempting to ask "why?" and to want to understand why something is the way it is, especially if you are an analytical person. However, you can often get all the communicative benefits of learning a new phrase without necessarily knowing the grammar that lies behind the phrase.

In fact, I have found that learning useful set phrases is extremely helpful, because it exposes you to natural grammar regardless of whether you understand the grammar or not. Over time, you find that the grammar from the phrases you have learnt begins to make sense to you, even though you may never have analysed it. I describe this as "free grammar" and it is far more effective than carrying out a deep analysis of everything you learn at the beginner stages - there are other more important activities to be doing!

The purpose of this chapter has been to show you the fundamental building blocks of French grammar that allow you to understand the most basic workings of the language, so you can begin to understand and speak French yourself. Needless to say, there is far more to French grammar than the contents of this chapter, and I fully expect you to have further questions about grammar at this stage.

One of the biggest mistakes made by students of foreign languages is to place too much importance on grammar in the early stages of learning. This is not to diminish the importance of grammar, but rather to say that grammar does not have to be mastered at the beginning. As a beginner, unable to read or understand much in French, the only way you can learn grammar is by studying abstract rules. However, once you can read and understand French you will be able to learn grammar naturally - as you find it being used in the real world - which gives you a far deeper understanding of the grammar than if you had learnt it as "rules", and also happens to be far easier.

When learners place too much importance on grammar at the beginner stages, and insist on "getting it right" before moving on, there is a significant danger of paralysis in learning. I have seen so many people fall out of love with a language simply because they develop a negative mindset towards grammar, frustrated by the number of rules to learn and the exceptions to those rules. With the grammar you have learnt in this chapter, you are already equipped not only to understand basic French, but also to make simple sentences yourself. Above all, with just a basic knowledge of grammar you can already make yourself understood, and that is the key - get started today and the rest will come with time!

Chapter 18 - The French Past Tenses

So far, we have really only given examples of French verbs in the present tense, but there exists a number of other tenses that you need to understand. Again, starting with the absolute basics, what is a tense? In English, French and many other languages, verbs change their forms depending on when the action of the verb takes place. For example, "eat" is the present tense while "ate" is the past tense. French actually has far more tenses than English for expressing notions of time but fortunately, you will not need to learn them all from the beginning. Some of the tenses are very uncommon or even obsolete, and you would be able to speak fluent French without ever learning them.

At the beginning, there are only a few tenses you will need to learn in order to express yourself in most everyday situations, and since you already know the present tense, the next most important tense to cover is the past tense. Here, we are going to discuss two forms of the past tense: the perfect and the imperfect, or *parfait* and *imparfait* in French.

These two tenses are used to talk about the past in French and differ somewhat from English past tenses. When talking about the past in French, there is one important distinction to make:

- an event that occurred just once, at a single point in time (e.g. a wedding)

- something that was true for an extended period of time (e.g. employment) or that happened regularly (e.g. holidays)

While English has an array of ways to express this, in French it is much simpler.

The Perfect Tense

In basic terms, the perfect tense is used to talk about a single event that took place in the past once. Examples of this in English would be:

- I ate the sandwich

- I saw the boy

To form the perfect tense in French, you need two different parts. The first part is known as the "auxiliary verb" and is usually (but not always) the verb *avoir*, "to have". The second part is the "past participle", a special past form of the main verb.

- *Auxiliary Verb + Past participle*

By combining these two parts, you get the perfect tense:

[18.1]

- j'ai mangé - I ate (je + ai = j'ai)

- tu as mangé - you ate

- il/elle a mangé - he/she ate

- nous avons mangé - we ate

- vous avez mangé - you (pl.) ate

- ils/elles ont mangé - they ate

Note that the perfect tense in French is formed in the same way as the present perfect in English and you may have spotted the similarity:

- I have *eaten*

- j'ai *mangé*

However, take care, because the usage is not the same. In English, the present perfect is used, among other things, to show that an action that took place in the past has some kind of connection to the present: *"I have eaten (and now I am full)"*. The French perfect does not have this meaning. The perfect tense in French only describes an action that took place in the past once and is now complete.

Before we move on from the perfect tense, it should be pointed out that not all French verbs take *avoir* as their auxiliary verb. Thirteen very common verbs, mostly related to movement, use the verb *être* ("to be") as an auxiliary. This means that "he came" in French is *il* est *venu* and not **il a venu*. This exception is actually easier than it seems because the verbs affected are quite common, you will quickly get the hang of it. For a complete list of verbs that take *être* in the perfect tense, see Appendix 4. Otherwise, simply be aware that these exceptions exist, and you will soon spot them in everyday French!

The Imperfect Tense

In contrast with the perfect tense in French is the imperfect tense, which has no equivalent in English. It is known as a "simple" tense since it is formed with the main verb itself and requires no auxiliary verb. In basic terms, the imperfect tense describes something in the past something that:

- was true for an extended period of time, or

- that happened regularly

Let's look at an example to make this clearer. Using the perfect tense, which you learnt in the last section, you might say *j'ai fumé une cigarette* - "I smoked a cigarette". This means that you smoked a cigarette, *one* cigarette, and now the cigarette is finished. In contrast, you may wish to say *"I used to smoke"*, in the sense of *"I used to be a smoker and I smoked cigarettes regularly"*. In that case, you would use the imperfect tense: *je fumais* - "I smoked/used to smoke". It was a situation in the past that remained true for a period of time.

Another use of the imperfect tense is to express the idea that one thing was happening when something else subsequently happened. Look at the following example, in which the verbs are bolded:

- Je conduisais ma voiture quand j'ai vu le garçon - I was driving my car when I saw the boy

In this sentence *je conduisais* is in the imperfect to express the idea of "I was driving", it was a continuous action that was taking place at that time. *J'ai vu le garçon* is in the perfect tense because it was a single event that took place and was completed.

In this section, you have learnt a simplified explanation of the perfect and imperfect tenses in order to demonstrate the main differences between the two tenses. If these ideas seem confusing right now, there is no need to worry, since you will soon become accustomed to the usage when you see the two tenses being used together. For now, the important thing is that you are aware of the difference between the perfect and the imperfect, how they are used, and are able to recognise their structure. Despite the differences with English, you will become accustomed to French tenses quite quickly once you see them in action! Lastly, spare a thought for native French speakers who learn English, as our complicated English tense system is far harder to get to grips with!

Chapter 19 - Introducing the Subjunctive

What is the Subjunctive?

Have you ever wondered why, in English, we say "God *save* the Queen" and not "God *saves* the Queen" or "it is important that you *be* there" rather than "it is important that you *are* there"? The reason is that these are rare examples of English using the *subjunctive*. While English has almost entirely lost its subjunctive, French still makes common use of this form, and it has been known to cause mild terror among some learners approaching an intermediate level of French. The main reason for fear of the subjunctive, at least for native English speakers, is our unfamiliarity with the subjunctive as a grammatical concept. However, as you will see, the subjunctive in French is actually fairly straightforward to understand and use.

So, what is the subjunctive? The subjunctive is known grammatically as a *mood* rather than a tense, and in French it is now used mainly in a number of expressions involving a feeling of doubt, desire, fear, or necessity. Again, this probably sounds a little abstract, so let's have a look at some examples. First of all, there are a certain number of common verbs which when followed by *que* ("that"), require a subjunctive:

[19.1]

- vouloir que - want
- souhaiter que - wish
- préférer que - prefer
- il faut que - must
- il est nécessaire que - it is necessary
- il semble que - it seems
- avoir peur que...(ne) - be afraid

To take *vouloir* ("want") as an example, in English you can say "I want you to go" but in French this construction is not possible. In French, you have to say "I want that you go" which gives you "*je veux que tu ailles*". In a normal sentence, "you go" is *tu vas* but here, because we must use the subjunctive, *tu vas* becomes *tu ailles*, the subjunctive form of the verb *aller*, "to go".

As well as these verbs, there are also a number of common conjunctions which require a subjunctive verb. Some examples are:

[19.2]

- bien que - although
    - Bien que tu saches - Although you know

- jusqu'à ce que - until

    - Jusqu'à ce que tu partes - Until you leave

- quoi que - whatever

    - Quoi que je fasse - Whatever I do

There are several others but the list is not long. You will soon realise that many of these expressions are both common and useful, making them easy to remember.

Olly's Tip:

When I first encountered the subjunctive in French, I remember thinking it would be really tough to remember how and when to use it. In reality, learning the subjunctive was quite easy. The reason is that, unlike a language like Spanish where the subjunctive is used liberally, the subjunctive in French is mostly used within a set phrase or with a small number of verbs. For example, a common way to say "you have to" in French is il faut que, *and with this phrase you must use the subjunctive:* il faut que tu ailles *("you have to go").*

Although this may look complicated at first glance, what I discovered is that I needed to use this phrase so often when speaking French

> that it quickly became second nature to use the subjunctive with whatever verb I needed: "you have to go/think/remember, etc." The trick is to pay attention to the relatively small number of expressions and verbs that take the subjunctive, and you will be fine!

Now let's look at how to form the subjunctive. Here again, we have some good news: the forms of the present subjunctive are not wildly different from the regular forms and are easy to remember with a little practice:

[19.3 - 19.5]

1st conjugation

Parler - to speak

- je parle
- tu parles
- il/elle parle
- nous parlions
- vous parliez
- ils/elles parlent

2nd conjugation

Vendre - to sell

- je vende
- tu vendes
- il/elle vende
- nous vendions
- vous vendiez
- ils/elles vendent

3rd conjugation

Finir - to finish

- je finisse
- tu finisses
- il/elle finisse
- nous finissions
- vous finissiez
- ils/elles finissent

You will notice that, especially for the 1st conjugation, many of the forms are the same as the regular forms and there are really only a few new ones to learn. You should be aware that some of the most common French verbs have an irregular subjunctive form, such as the form for *aller* ("to go") we saw earlier, where *tu vas* ("you go") becomes *tu ailles* in the subjunctive. However, rather than learning these irregular subjunctive forms in advance, they are best left until later when you encounter them individually.

Now that you understand what the subjunctive is, and that the subjunctive is used with particular phrases and verbs in French, your brain will have become primed to notice them when they appear. You will also see that the irregular subjunctive verb forms tend to stick out for being quite different from any other verb forms, which only makes them easier to spot! For a brief list of irregular subjunctive forms, see Appendix 5.

There is one last aspect of the subjunctive that we need to mention. So far, we have been discussing only the relatively common present subjunctive but in fact there are three other subjunctive forms in French:

- the imperfect subjunctive

- the perfect subjunctive

- the pluperfect subjunctive

Before you throw your hands up in despair, of these three, only the perfect subjunctive is in use in spoken French, and even that only very rarely. The other two are practically obsolete in daily life and are restricted to literary use. If you intend to study academic French or read highbrow French literature, you will certainly have to learn about these different subjunctive forms. If you are just interested in everyday French, though, you can forget all about them.

In normal, everyday spoken French, even the present subjunctive is considered to belong to a slightly higher register of speech, and in informal conversation people usually express things in other more colloquial ways.

Chapter 20 - French Prepositions

Prepositions are a particular *bête noire* for language learners of just about any language as each language has its own set of prepositions which generally do not correspond exactly to other languages, even closely related ones. This is a topic that can - and often does - fill long chapters of grammar books. Therefore, sticking to the methodology of this book, where you learn only the essentials in order to get started, this chapter will be a brief (yet robust) introduction to the wonderful world of prepositions in French.

What Are Prepositions?

Prepositions are small words that link together all the other words in a sentence, and tell you where things happen, why they happen or when they happen. The following words are prepositions in English:

- in
- on
- at
- by

There are many more! Prepositions are words that you rarely think about in English - except, of course, when you want to know how to express them in a foreign language.

Take an innocent-looking word like "for" for example. You might not imagine expressing such a simple idea in French would present any problems but it depends what you mean by "for". If you have a gift "for" someone, you might use *à*, but *pour* might also be appropriate in certain contexts. If you want to express the length of time you have been doing a certain activity, you will use *depuis* ("since"), but if that activity is now finished and in the past, you then need to choose *pendant* ("during"). If you want to say you are doing something "for" someone, you can use *pour*, but if you want to swap something "for" something else, you can use either *pour* ("for") or *contre* ("against"). All of a sudden, our seemingly benign preposition "for" is not looking quite so innocent!

There really is no effective way to study your way through the challenge of mastering prepositions. As usual, the solution lies in plenty of exposure to French and actively noticing the usage of prepositions when you find them. We have mentioned the words "exposure" and "noticing" already a few times in this chapter, and they really are the key to much of the success you will find in language learning. By continually paying attention to the French you find in textbooks, short stories, or spoken by native speakers on the street, and asking yourself why a certain preposition has been used, you will give your brain the best chance of learning them naturally.

Olly's Tip:

When you notice a preposition being used in a French sentence, and the preposition was not what you expected, try repeating the entire sentence aloud a few times. Conscious repetition helps to crystallise new language in your brain, and saying aloud something you have head strengthens your memory.

There are two French prepositions in particular - *à* and *de* - which will be helpful to discuss at this stage, as they have the tendency to cause confusion in the early stages of learning French.

The Preposition À

À is one of the most common prepositions in French and is closely related to the English "at":

- à l'école - at school
- à midi - at midday

However, *à* can also mean "for":

- un verre à bière - a glass for beer or in more natural English, "a beer glass" (un verre de bière is "a glass of beer")

Finally, in a case that often turns up in school exam papers, à can also mean "on":

- à la télé - on TV

The Preposition *De*

De is closest to the English "of" (as we just saw with the beer glass) and is used to form the French possessive, as in:

- le portable de Françoise - the mobile of Françoise or in more natural English, "Françoise's mobile".

However, *de* can also mean "from":

- il est revenu de Chine - he has come back from China

Finally, *de* may also be used to mean "with" or "in":

- couvert de sang - covered with/in blood

In the examples above of *à* and *de,* I have given the closest English equivalent in order to highlight the variety in usage of these prepositions. However, what you may have noticed is that there is only a limited amount of overlap in the meanings of prepositions in French and English, and this is an important realisation. We all have a tendency to translate in order to make sense of new vocabulary, and this is not a bad thing. In fact, translation is often very helpful as a language learning technique.

However, in the case of French prepositions, which are so uniquely *French*, and where translation is so problematic, the lesson is to avoid translations from the start. By all means refer to a translation in order to understand the core meaning of a new phrase, such as *un verre à bière* ("a beer glass" or "a glass for beer") which is not intuitive for English speakers, but do not attempt to understand why *à* is being used to mean "for" in this sentence, because... it does not mean "for" at all! Simply learn the preposition along with the sentence you found it in, in order to keep the context present at all times. Usually, the meaning of a preposition is easy to figure out from the context as long as you know some of the other words in the sentence.

The difficulty can come when you need to choose the correct preposition to use yourself in order to construct a sentence, but this comes with time. Looking for hard and fast rules for prepositions will let you down, as anyone who has been through the journey of learning French will tell you. Absorb prepositions naturally by hearing and seeing them in context, rather than learning rules for their usage.

How to Approach Grammar - My Conclusion

At the start of Chapter 11, we discussed the fact that grammar is not as useful as vocabulary in getting your point across - words themselves convey more meaning than the grammar used to string them together. In fact, by some estimates, up to 95% of all meaning in a language is conveyed by the words themselves, which leaves only 5% of meaning to be made up by grammar. What I would like you to take from this statistic is an important lesson for your language learning mindset: grammar is not the most important part of language learning.

This is not to diminish the importance of grammar, but to caution against grammar study becoming your main activity - something which is all too common in language classrooms across the world. This often comes as a wake-up call for learners, as you may well have memories of language learning at school involving predominantly grammar practice. For a beginner especially, grammar is important, but not as important as vocabulary. For every 30 minutes you spend learning grammar, try to spend at least an hour (preferably more) reading and listening to French, whether from passages of dialogue in your textbook or other sources.

Similarly, when you do encounter a grammar rule, whether in this book or in other textbooks, the best approach is to take a cursory look at the rule and then simply go off to look for that grammar being used naturally in other places - it is by *noticing* French grammar being used in the real world that you will come to truly understand how the grammar is used. In that sense, a grammar book is best used as reference material to search for grammar explanations as and when something interesting appears naturally during your studies. Grammar books should not be the primary source of your learning - look things up when you are interested and ready to do so.

The main task of this book has been to introduce you to all the main grammatical concepts in French you need to know to get started, precisely so that you can now start to consume real French material and not feel at a loss to understand basic grammar. There will of course be many unknown words in the material you study, but those words are precisely that - vocabulary, not grammar.

Olly's Tip:

Learning a new language inevitably means dealing with ambiguity. Even when you become more advanced in a language, there will always be words, grammar and other concepts you struggle to understand. One of the major lessons I have learnt through learning successive languages has been that the happier you are to live with a bit of ambiguity, especially at the beginning, and especially with grammar, the more successful you will be in the long run. Be content with not understanding everything right now; it all comes with time, and you will have a happier learning experience as a result.

Part 5: Your French Learning Routine

Chapter 20 - Creating a Simple Learning Plan

Learning How to Learn

You have probably heard that learning your first foreign language is always the hardest and that each subsequent language is easier than the last. This is not because your brain somehow becomes stronger, like when you exercise a muscle, although this may be true to some extent. Rather, the reason is more to do with the fact that experienced language learners discover *how* to learn a language. Through trial and error, learning one language after the next, it becomes apparent what is effective for the learner and, just as importantly, what is not effective for them.

Notice the two little words at the end of the last sentence - *for them*. When we talk about what is effective in language learning, it may be a cliché, but it is absolutely true to say that every person is different and learns languages in different ways, and this goes for every aspect of the learning process. Such variables might include: how long to study for every day, how to learn vocabulary, whether to practise with native speakers and how often, what kind of textbooks to use, taking formal language classes or private lessons, watching movies with or without subtitles, doing the exercises in your textbook or not... the list is endless!

The only way to become a successful language learner is to discover what works for you one step at a time. Having said that, it can help to take inspiration from others who have successfully learned languages, and there exists a certain amount of "best practice" in language learning which can help you get off to a good start and avoid common mistakes. As such, in the following sections I will give some of the language learning advice that has worked best for me in the past, and that I know has resonated with my students and readers. To the extent that this advice provides a model to follow as you begin to discover your own learning style it should prove useful.

Start with Your Motivation for Learning French

Learning French is a long-term undertaking and part of the challenge facing any learner is to remain motivated beyond the first few weeks and throughout the whole process. At the beginning, learning a new language is fresh and exciting and you will make rapid progress. However, as the first weeks turn into months, you can expect to feel your initial progress slow a little and you may lose sight of why you started learning French in the first place. In moments like this, you need to find ways to rekindle your enthusiasm and remember why you originally decided to start learning French.

Therefore, when you first start out, it is a good idea to be specific about your motivations. Think about why you want to learn French. Is it because it will help your career? Do you have a particular attachment to France? Do you live in France and want to integrate better with the community? What are the specific benefits you look forward to in your life once you can speak French? It is a good idea to jot down a list of your reasons for learning French, so that when the inevitable moment of disillusionment arrives, you can come back to your list to reengage with your core motivations.

Set Specific Goals

Once you have clearly articulated your reasons for learning French, it will help you to set a long-term language goal. Whatever stage you are at in learning a language, without a goal of some kind how will you ever know when you have succeeded? When setting your goal, try to be more specific than simply: "I will speak French fluently!" I like to express my goals in terms of what I will be able to do, rather than a notional idea of fluency. Goals expressed in this way might look like:

- I will be able to watch and enjoy a French film without subtitles by Christmas

- I will be able to go on holiday to France next summer and get by without English

- I will pass my B1-level exam in February

Having some kind of goal articulated will give you something more concrete to work towards than simply "learn French", be a source of motivation, and help you make better decisions about your learning.

Your Core Daily French Practice

We have looked at a variety of techniques and tips for learning French in this book, but how much and how often should you actually study? I have learnt that success in language learning depends largely on being consistent, and that going for days (or even weeks) without studying makes it difficult to progress. Therefore, I try to make language learning a part of my lifestyle and this means aiming to study every day. Now, in reality, I do take days off - sometimes a few days off! However, when you consider that learning a language is a long-term project, it seems smarter to set out with the intention of studying every day and to allow yourself some flexibility within that, than to do the opposite, which is to "fit it in" wherever you have time.

To make sure language learning is part of my lifestyle, I have a daily *core study time*. This is a session of around 45 minutes (sometimes more, sometimes less) which I like to do first thing in the morning, before my day begins. Having my *core study time* early in the morning helps make sure the study gets done, because once the working day begins it is hard to carve out time for anything else! I sit in a quiet room where I will not be distracted and I use the time to do what you might call the "hard work" - concentrated and focused study, as opposed to activities such as browsing language videos on YouTube, which is usually a shallow activity full of distraction.

Now, the key is to make your *core study time* regular, because it is in the act of revisiting the language every day that you learn new things and deepen your understanding of what you already know. Along with consistency, the other most important aspect of this approach to learning languages is the creation of time for in-depth study. You may have plenty of dead time throughout your day - on the bus, during your lunch hour - and this can be useful time for extra practice, but dead time is often short and prone to distraction. I have found nothing to be as valuable as quiet, uninterrupted time for language learning in which you can truly focus, and that is why I create this *core study time* every day and make it a priority.

What I have described here is the routine that works particularly well for me - I can focus well in the morning, and 45-60 minutes is a productive amount of time. However, I would be the first to say you should adapt this to fit your personal preferences. If the most practical and productive study time for you is 15 minutes in the evening before bed, then that is precisely what you should do. The important thing is to study consistency and to create an environment in which you can focus.

Finding Time to Speak

We have touched on the importance of speaking French throughout this book, and in Chapter 22 I will provide some practical suggestions for finding good speaking partners. The way I view speaking practice is not so much for learning new things (although you certainly will), but rather to consolidate what you have already learnt. Speaking with people is your opportunity to take the language you have learnt on your own and put it into practice, so that speaking starts to become natural and you learn to express yourself better in French. Once you feel ready to start speaking and have experienced your first conversations in French, you may well become addicted to the feeling of communicating in another language, which is a wonderful thing!

However, the practicalities of creating the time to speak French with people is not always easy, and for this reason there is an ongoing risk that you go for weeks or months without speaking with anyone, for no reason other than you do not get around to organising it. Unless you are lucky enough to be surrounded by French speakers, you will have to be proactive in creating your own opportunities to speak French. In my own learning, I realised a long time ago that if I do not schedule my speaking time, it will not happen! Therefore, I have a rule of scheduling multiple lessons and language exchanges at a time, usually deciding on the next four or five dates in advance, so that they go into my diary and are fixed. As a consequence, my speaking happens. I recommend you do the same.

Studying in Your Dead Time

If you have adopted the principle of *core study time*, then you are off to a great start. The good news, though, is that there is almost certainly plenty of extra time throughout your day which you can take advantage of to spend more time with French. *Dead time* refers to those moments in the day when you cannot be productive and have no choice but to wait. Commuting is the classic example, but you may also spend time walking, eating, or waiting for meetings to start. People use this time differently, but there is a fair chance that in such situations you either reach for your phone, daydream, or some combination of the two!

Periods of dead time throughout your day can add up to considerable amounts of time - easily an hour or more per day - and this time can be a great asset for your language learning if you make use it in smart way. While your *core study time* is best used for focused study, your dead time is ideal for less intense, more entertaining activities. For most people, the trick to taking advantage of your dead time is to use your smartphone or tablet to make your language learning material portable. By all means, you can carry your textbook around with you all day, but technology has given us many options for accessing the material we want anywhere:

- Download podcasts in French

- Use electronic flashcards to review your vocabulary

- Read the news in French on *Le Monde* website

- Buy French short story books for your Kindle (I have a written series of short story books for beginners which are referenced at the start of this book.)

- Take pictures on your phone of the chapter you are currently working on in your textbook so you always have it with you

- Take a picture of the grammar tables you are trying to memorise

The great thing about using your dead time to study French is that everyone has dead time, it does not have to be scheduled, and it can quickly add up to large amounts of time. The trick is to develop the habit of recognising when you are at a loose end and to use the time for French rather than Facebook!

What Should the First Year of French Look Like?

Let's imagine you have a goal of achieving a good level of proficiency in French in one year. What would that year look like, and how would you need to study differently over the course of that year in order to reach your goal? This is a frequently-asked question which is helpful for developing the mindset of a good language learner, and so in this closing section I will describe my experience of how the study process changes as your level improves.

Getting Started: The First Three Months

At the beginning you know little or no French, and so your first task is to learn the basics. It is helpful to gain as complete a picture as possible of the basics of the language, and the best way to do that is to work quickly through an entry-level book such as this from cover to cover, spending your time listening to the sounds of the language, and looking at the basic explanations of grammar. It is preferable to be fairly superficial at this stage, as the value lies in getting a general picture of the language rather than memorising every detail.

After this, you will need to move on to a more complete textbook that will give you a good grounding in all aspects of

French, including pronunciation, vocabulary, grammar and so on. The majority of your time should be spent listening and reading to the dialogues in the textbook, referring to grammar explanations where necessary to help you understand the contents of the dialogues. (You will learn the most French by reading and listening, not by learning rules.)

At this stage, you should start to learn any key verbs, useful expressions and basic verb conjugations that you have not yet mastered, as these will allow you to start speaking and communicating with people. At the same time, I recommend starting to work with a teacher or language partner, and the best way to use your speaking time is to practise the material you have learnt from your textbook.

This is an exciting phase in which you learn a lot, quickly, and your progress is tangible.

Building on Your Foundations: Months 3-6

At this stage, you should have a strong foundation in French and be able to hold a basic conversation on simple topics. This next phase might last for another three months, but will feel very different to the first phase: at this point, despite having studied for a few months already, you will still struggle to understand spoken French, and you will grow frustrated at not being able to express yourself as well as you would like.

The main goal of this phase is to grow your vocabulary as much and as fast as possible, because without enough *words* you will not be able to speak or understand enough to hold enjoyable conversations. In order to grow your vocabulary, you need to give yourself as much exposure as possible to French, and this means doing a lot of listening and reading. The problem you face in doing this, however, is that your comprehension is not yet good enough to read interesting content; you will struggle with newspapers, novels, radio, or any material intended for native speakers. Therefore, you will likely be restricted to learner material such as intermediate level textbooks or graded readers, and may have to compromise on the "fun factor"!

It is also vital at this stage to begin to speak more. I recommend at least three speaking sessions a week of 30-60 minutes, but ideally more. In these speaking sessions, you should talk about a variety of topics, and it is helpful to use your study material as inspiration for this. For example, if you have been reading a story about World War II, you can discuss the story with your speaking partner, which allows you to review the new vocabulary you have learnt, and gain more and more confidence in your speaking.

Pushing on Towards Fluency: From Month Six Onwards

After around six months of regular study, you should have developed a good conversational level in French, and now be able to understand a fair amount - although you will still feel out of your depth when given native-level material. At this stage, you will want to move away from *studying* the language and start *using* it in your daily life, with real people and for real purposes. You will still find it hard, but this is the stage where you need to take a step up, and learn by doing.

Your aim for this period is to do everything possible to integrate French into your daily life. Attend events where people speak French, join French Meetup groups, watch TV in French instead of in English, read the news in French rather than English, read magazines and books. In short, replace everything you normally do in English with French. The more immersion you can create for yourself, the faster and more effective your learning will be. When choosing material to read, the guiding principle is to choose things you are genuinely interested in. If you like cycling, read French books on cycling. If you like healthy eating, read blogs or watch YouTube channels that talk about healthy eating in French. There is no greater source of motivation than spending your time doing things that interest you.

Finally, you may consider using more advanced tools such as a frequency dictionary. This is a dictionary that lists words in French in their order of frequency in daily life. When browsing through the dictionary, any unknown words you encounter will be the most useful for you to learn. In this way, you can use the frequency dictionary to "plug the holes" in your French. You might also study an advanced grammar textbook, for example, in order to improve your grammar in a targeted way. Perhaps ironically, the more advanced you get, the more you will find studying grammar to be useful.

This phase lasts longer than the other two phases combined, the reason being that mastering the most advanced areas of a language is inevitably harder than learning the basics. In this phase, you shift your approach to learning French dramatically, away from *studying* and towards *living* the language.

If you can follow the spirit of this three-phase structure for a year, you will find yourself with a good level of French, able to cope well in daily life, and fully able to meet new people and make friends. I hope this prospect is exciting for you - it should be! Of course, for many people, doing this in one year will be too intensive, but the balance of the journey looks the same whether you do it in one year or ten years.

Olly's Tip:

Every time I learn a foreign language the experience is different, and my progress is never as clear-cut as I have made cut above! Having said that, in order to reach fluency in my languages, I have always had to pass through these three phases at some point. Take these three phases more as inspiration than prescription - simply being aware that the language learning process does change and morph in this way will become useful to you at some point in the future when you recognise you have reached a new phases in your own learning!

Chapter 21 - Seven Mistakes to Avoid as a Beginner

Here are some tips for avoiding some of the most common mistakes made when learning French:

1. Do Not Learn Lists of Vocabulary

Anyone who learnt a language at school will probably remember learning lists of words for vocabulary tests. As we have already discussed, learning French does involve acquiring large amounts of new words, but the key word here is acquiring - not learning by rote for a test. Acquiring vocabulary means not only knowing the true meaning of a word (and how to use it), but also knowing the word for the long-term. Learning lists of vocabulary can be effective for putting words in your short-term memory - long enough to remember for your test - but a week or two later most of the vocabulary will have disappeared from your memory. Furthermore, learning individual vocabulary items is disadvantageous, because there is no context to tell you how to use the words naturally. This means that even if you do manage to memorise words from lists, you are unlikely to know the true meaning of those words or how to use them. Resist the temptation to slip into old habits, and approach the task of learning vocabulary by getting a rich diet of spoken and written French. Apply the principle of the ART Technique from Chapter 14 to guide new vocabulary into your long-term memory.

2. Do Not Rely on Translation

A certain amount of translation in language learning is inevitable, but an overreliance on translating between French and English can prevent you from learning to think in French. When you listen to spoken French, try not to search for word-for-word equivalences in English. Instead, try to listen to complete sentences and figure out the meaning that the speaker is trying to convey. This will not always be possible, especially at the very beginning, but it is a good habit to get into because, over time, it reduces the "panic" many learners feel when they encounter a difficult word in conversation. If you are used to thinking in French, and not relying on the English translation, you will develop skills that will help you understand spoken French even without knowing every word that is used. When you learn new French words, try to learn them as they are, without "attaching" them to an English meaning. In any case, many words cannot be translated precisely and later you will even find you know words in French that you do not know how to say in English!

3. Do Not Look Up Everything in the Dictionary

Have you considered that there are many words in English you do not know? (It is, after all, impossible to know all words in a language!) There are also times when you may not hear a word clearly, which amounts to the same thing as not knowing the word. In these cases, in spite of dealing with an unknown word, you are almost always able to understand the overall meaning of what the speaker is saying, and you certainly do not panic! You should have the same aim in French - you do not need to know every word in a sentence in order to understand the meaning. For this reason, the habit of reaching for the dictionary every time you hear a new word is unhelpful, as it brings you back to trying to understand each word in a sentence, rather than developing your guessing skills!

4. Do Not Be Afraid to Open Your Mouth and Make Mistakes

Making mistakes is a very important part of the learning process and every time you make a mistake, you improve. If you wait until you can speak French perfectly before you start speaking, you will never start speaking. You may feel a little reluctant to speak because you think you will be judged for the mistakes you make. This is simply not true and the majority of people are very happy to see people trying to speak their language, and are usually very encouraging and glad to help. The biggest danger of all is to allow speaking to become a source of fear, because then you may avoid speaking with people altogether. For most people, being able to speak French is a major motivation for learning, so do not avoid opportunities to speak and practise, and embrace the prospect of making mistakes as being your best teacher!

5. Do Not Write Everything Down

You do not need to write everything down or take notes of every new French word or phrase you hear. Maybe notetaking was encouraged at school - but this is a good opportunity to reflect on previous experiences and to examine their effectiveness. Now, there is certainly value to writing things down as part of any learning process, but it is important to acknowledge the fact that most language notebooks simply gather dust on the shelf - if you write down a new word, will you *really* go back and review it later? If you have a structured study process that involves systematically reviewing the contents of your old notebook, then you may find value in taking extensive notes. In many cases, it is probably more efficient to be selective about the notes you take, and restrict your notes to words, phrases, passages of texts, or ideas that you consider to be too valuable to miss! Remember that there is a cost to taking notes: your *attention*. The cost of taking notes is to not be focusing on the language in front of you. There is a danger that you do not fully engage with a conversation if you are too preoccupied with taking notes, and that your brain will not try hard to find ways to remember information if you know it is written down in your notebook. As usual, it is a question of balance, but from time to time, try putting the pen down and simply focusing on the language.

6. Do Not Try to Remember Everything

In language learning, you will forget a lot more than you will learn. Do not try to remember everything first time, as it will only slow your learning down to a snail's pace and cause undue stress. New vocabulary will be remembered over time with practice. If it helps, you have my full permission to forget new words and phrases! Your learning will be much faster as a result, for a number of reasons. Firstly, you will discover as you progress that many of the things you wanted to learn as a beginner were probably not necessary to learn after all! Secondly, your brain will remember certain things without any effort, but only if it has the opportunity to see them in the first place. If you avoid getting bogged-down and keep moving through your learning material, you will cover more ground and allow your brain to learn the "low-hanging fruit" without having to expend much effort. Some things must be learnt, of course, and so the golden rule is to be selective about what you spend your time memorising, as we covered in Chapter 12, and to ignore the vocabulary about seafaring in the 19th Century!

7. Do Not Worry Too Much About Accent

As with grammar, accent is another area that has a tendency to get learners of French tied up in knots and can be a source of considerable anxiety. French pronunciation (as distinct from accent) is vitally important and is one of the few areas where an insistence on getting it right at the beginning pays off later. With that said, you will be unlikely to ever develop a perfect French accent, indistinguishable from a native speaker. (You can review the difference between accent and pronunciation in Chapter 10.) As a beginner, your priority should be to develop clear and intelligible pronunciation in French - nothing more. If the person you are speaking to understands you without strain, that is good enough. You must not let anxiety over your accent prevent you from enjoying speaking the language and communicating with French people. Your perfect Parisian accent can wait!

Chapter 22 - Five Things to Get Right as a Beginner

In the last chapter, we looked at some common mistakes to avoid when learning French as a beginner. Now, let's look at the five steps I recommend you follow in order to get off to the best possible start learning French.

1. Find a Good Teacher

While it is perfectly possible to learn a language through self-study, and many independent language learners do so, I recommend that you find yourself a good teacher when you begin learning French, especially if this is your first foreign language. A good teacher will help provide some structure to your learning, give you feedback on your mistakes, encourage you, and, most importantly, help fine-tune your pronunciation. For many students, simply having another human being to interact and practise speaking French with is enough to provide a motivational boost.

What makes a good teacher? A good teacher is somebody who can help you learn faster than you might be able to on your own. He or she should be encouraging and create an environment in which you feel comfortable speaking French without worrying about making mistakes. Your teacher should allow you to have a say in what you learn, and in the material you use, and treat your lesson time as much as a conversation as a formal class. They should occasionally correct your grammar and pronunciation, but not too much - allowing you the opportunity to speak freely without interruption is also important. Lastly, your teacher does not necessarily have to be a native French speaker. In my experience, many of the best language teachers are non-native speakers of a language; their experience of learning the language themselves can give them a special insight into your learning journey.

Finding the kind of teacher described above might sound like a tall order, but I assure you that you will know it when you find her! I am often asked how to spot a good teacher and this description will give you some points to consider. In addition to local listings and adverts for language teachers, you should also consider taking lessons online, as they offer you much more flexibility in scheduling and can also be more affordable.

Olly's Tip:

There are many websites you can use to find French teachers online, but the company I recommend and use personally is Italki, who allow you to choose from both informal tutors and professional teachers. For special offers, and other options for finding affordable speaking practice, please visit my resource page at : http://iwillteachyoualanguage.com /resources

2. Learn Key Phrases and Important Verbs

As we said before, learning lists of words as a general language learning strategy will get you nowhere, but there is significant value in learning the most common French words and phrases at the beginning. Why? For two reasons: firstly, because learning common words and phrases will allow you to start communicating; secondly, because these words and phrases are so common that you will encounter them everywhere and quickly learn to use them naturally without much effort.

Learning set phrases sometimes involves learning grammatical constructions that you do not yet understand, such as in the phrase: *Qu'est-ce que c'est?* - "What is it?", which may appear terrifying to a beginner! However, there is a world of difference between understanding the grammar of a phrase, and simply using the phrase in order to get what you want. You do not need to understand the mechanics of why you say something in a certain way. Indeed, "why" may not always be a helpful question to ask when there is material to learn! If a phrase appears to be useful, then simply learn the phase as-is.

Examples of other potential confusing, yet extremely important, expressions might be:

- Je m'appelle... - My name is...

- Est-ce que vous pouvez... ? - Can you...? (asking someone to do something)

- Est-ce que je peux... ? - Can I...? (asking if you are allowed to do something)

You can find a full list of the essential French phrases I suggest you start with in Appendix 1 at the end of this book. Be sure to use the Audio Vault to check your pronunciation.

3. Learn the Fundamentals

Perhaps you have bad memories of learning a language at school, where after sitting through years of French classes you were still barely able to string a sentence together. Learning a new language should never be like this, not least because you can make faster progress as a beginner than at any other stage of the language learning journey. Make the most of the energy and motivation you feel right now to get a good grounding in the fundamentals of French grammar - conveniently, everything that is covered in this book!

Some parts of French grammar, such as the conjugation of verbs in the present tense, are essential and must simply be memorised, since without the ability to conjugate basic verbs you will be unable to communicate in French. My core recommendation in this book, however, is that you do not stop there - you should familiarise yourself with all the main grammatical concepts in French right from the beginning, rather than waiting months for them to appear in a school syllabus. You may not need to use these concepts yourself for some time, but by becoming aware that the concepts exist you give yourself a more complete picture of the grammar of the language and prime your brain to learn grammar much more easily further down the line.

There is nothing as motivating as making quick progress as a beginner in a new language, and the sense of progress and achievement itself will encourage you to keep going. For this reason, the best time to work hard and learn the basics is at the start.

4. Get a Good French Textbook

It is commonly said that a language cannot be taught, it must be learnt. However good a teacher may be and however effectively they guide you in your learning, the desire to learn must exist within the student or nothing will be learnt at all. In other words, you must take responsibility for your learning, and in order to do this you need the right tools. Whether or not you have a French teacher, I strongly recommend you have a good self-study textbook so that you can learn independently: look up grammar, practise reading, learn new words, complete grammar drills, and so on, outside your lesson time.

Personally, when I learn a new language, the first challenge I set myself is always to work through a good textbook cover-to-cover before taking any lessons, in order to familiarise myself with the main concepts of the language. I find it is far more efficient to learn the basics in my own time, instead of hiring a teacher to essentially give me the same information I already have in my textbook.

When trying to find the right textbook for you, I suggest you take a trip to your local bookshop so you can physically look through a selection of titles. Here are a few things to consider:

- Determine which level of book you need. Language textbooks usually start with A1, for beginners, and go up to C2, for advanced students. Choose a book that covers a suitable range, and avoid the temptation to choose something too advanced.

- Why are you learning French? Do you want to learn the basics for a trip? Do you hope to use French for business? Are you aiming for all-around fluency? Knowing this will help you choose a suitable textbook, or avoid an unsuitable one!

- Look for a textbook with plenty of dialogues. You will have noticed that I have mentioned the importance of exposure to French many times in this book. The more input you receive via reading and listening the faster you will grow your vocabulary and break out of beginner French. Dialogues in textbooks are great for this because they (usually) give you examples of spoken French in realistic situations, that are not too difficult to understand. Ensure that the dialogues come with accompanying audio.

- Choose a book you like. This sounds like a trivial point, but many people will be tempted to learn French using a hand-me-down textbook, their old book from school, or something they found lying around the office! It is vitally important you actually like your chosen textbook, or else you will not look forward to picking it up every day to study with. Look at a variety of textbooks and choose one you find aesthetically pleasing and that you can imagine yourself working with on a daily basis.

Look inside the textbook first and see if the material is written in a straightforward way that is easy to understand. Make sure the book contains enough descriptive details that you feel you have all the information you need (some textbooks are nothing more than exercises, with no explanation). Lastly, you may also like to choose two different books, so you can see alternative explanations and switch between the two if you get bored.

5. Find French People to Speak With

The final and most important step in learning any language is to practise. You can study alone every day with a textbook for months, but this does not lead automatically to an ability to speak. Conversely, if you create regular opportunities to practise speaking French, even as a beginner, the confidence you will gain combined with the extra exposure to real spoken French, will turn you into a versatile speaker of French over time. I consider "speaking practice" to be distinct and separate from lessons with your teacher, because there is a different dynamic and you typically have to work harder to make the conversation successful.

To find people to practise French with you should look both online and in your local area. French meetup groups or societies are often a good place to start, especially if you live near a large town or city:

- Alliance Française: https://www.alliancefr.org/

- Meetup.com: https://www.meetup.com/

You might also simply search online for "French conversation" or "French language exchange" to see what pops up near you.

If you struggle to find options near you then you can use one of the many websites and apps which help you connect with language exchange partners online, through Skype calls or text chat. For a complete list, please visit my resource page:

- http://iwillteachyoualanguage.com/resources

Lastly, I run a private Facebook community for language enthusiasts, in which many people have found fantastic language exchange partners. You can join for free at:

- https://www.facebook.com/groups/fluencymastermind

- Or search on Facebook: fluency mastermind

The internet has revolutionised language learning and created countless opportunities that never existed before to practise with people from all over the world. If you are unfamiliar with these opportunities, I encourage you to look into the websites I have listed above, you may be pleasantly surprised! Connecting with real people to practise French with is the most enjoyable and human element of language learning, and there has never been a better time to get started!

Final Words on French

If you follow these simple steps, you will soon find that your French ability is improving exponentially. As anyone who has ever successfully learnt a foreign language can tell you, when you suddenly realise you are having a conversation in French, expressing yourself and understanding what is being said to you, it is an amazing feeling.

A little while ago, I received a question for my podcast from a 17-year-old in the UK called Ben. Ben asked whether he should bother learning another language, since there is so much technology that can help translate for us these days… and everyone speaks English anyway! I had to think about my answer carefully, because I felt like there was quite a lot at stake. Ben could quite easily not decide to learn a new language and go through life happily doing other things. On the other hand, I thought that if I could persuade him that learning a new language was indeed worth his while, he might end up taking the challenge and eventually living a life enriched in ways that he probably could not comprehend at his age.

When preparing my answer, I thought about many different arguments I could make in favour of language learning. I thought about mentioning the fact that if you learn another language you get to meet lots of people, or pointing to research that suggests that multilingual children's brains are larger. But those answers did not seem convincing enough. Instead, my thoughts kept returning to my experience living in Egypt some years ago. In Egypt there is a lot of poverty, and despite Egyptians being among the most friendly and warm-hearted people anywhere in the world, I found an unavoidable gap between myself and the people I would meet in the streets of Cairo.

However, after studying Arabic for a certain number of months, I reached a point where I was able to hold a conversation. My confidence improved, I began speaking more, and my experience in Cairo changed dramatically. Suddenly, when someone in the street would strike up a conversation with me in broken English and I was able to reply in Arabic, I would see the expression on their face transform before my eyes. It is difficult to know exactly what that person must feel in those moments, but based on the tirade of questions that would usually follow, and the invitations for food or tea, I would say it is a sense of happiness and pride that someone from outside has taken an interest in their culture and gone to the lengths of learning their language. It is considered a significant gesture and, for me personally, it is an enriching feeling like no other to be able to connect with people from such a different background in that way.

This is the story I told to Ben. I do not know whether I articulated my experiences very well when I recorded my reply. Perhaps he never even listened to my answer to his question!

However, learning a new language, for all the frustration it may cause you along the way, is the best way I know to cross borders and cultures, irrespective other events in the world, and to touch your own life and the lives of others in the most unexpected ways.

If you are curious, you can listen to my reply to Ben here: http://www.iwillteachyoualanguage.com/episode11/

When you are finished with listening to the recording, it is time to get started on your French - because we have some work to do!

- Olly

Part 6: Appendices & Resources

Appendix 1 - Useful Words & Expressions

[A1.1 - A1.108]

Useful Expressions

- Comment on dit ... en français ? - How do you say ... in French?

- Je (ne) comprends pas - I do not understand

- Je comprends - I understand

- ..., ça veut dire quoi ? - What does ... mean ?

- ..., qu'est-ce que ça veut dire ? - What does ... mean ?

    o Example : "je ne sais pas", ça veut dire quoi ? – I do not know, what does it mean ?

- Je (ne) sais pas comment on dit ça en français - I do not know how to say that in French

- Je (ne) sais pas comment on dit ... en français - I do not know how to say ... in French

- Je (ne) sais pas - I do not know

- Je sais - I know

- Peux-tu répéter (s'il te plaît) ? - Can you repeat that, please?

- Pouvez-vous répéter (s'il vous plaît) ? Can you repeat, please? (formal)

- Peux-tu répéter ça plus lentement (s'il te plaît) ? - Please say that again more slowly.

- Je (n')ai pas compris - I didn't understand

- J'ai oublié - I forgot

- D'accord/ok/ça va - Okay

- Comment ? (polite) - What?

- Quoi ? (familiar) - What?

- Attends ! - Wait!

- Je (ne) t'entends pas - I cannot hear you

- Tu peux l'écrire (s'il te plaît) ? - Can you write it, please?

- Comment on épelle …. en français ? - How do you spell … in French?

- Quoi de neuf ? – What's up?/What's new?/How is it going ?

- Tu peux me tutoyer - We can use "tu"/We can talk to each other informally

- On peut se tutoyer - We can use "tu"/We can talk to each other informally

- Tu viens d'où ? - Where do you come from?

- Je suis Anglais, Américain, Espagnol, ...- I'm English/American/Spanish

- On peut continuer la conversation en français s'il te plaît ? j'aimerais pratiquer un peu - Can we continue the conversation in French ? I would like to practice a bit

  Note: This is the most common way to ask this question to a friend. In written French, it would be *"Peut-on continuer la conversation en français s'il te plaît ?"*. If you want to be more formal/polite (when talking to a stranger for example), you can say: *"Est-ce qu'on pourrait continuer la conversation en français, s'il vous plaît ?"*

- Tu fais quoi dans la vie ? - What do you do for a living?

- Ça va ? - How are you?

- Ça va, et toi ? - I am fine, thank you.

- Je pense que ... - I think...

- Je veux dire que ... - I want to say...

Essential Verbs

- savoir - to know (a fact)
- connaître - to know (a person/place)
- manger - to eat
- boire - to drink
- dormir - to sleep
- se coucher - go to bed
- sortir - go out/leave
- rentrer - come/go home
- aller au travail - go to work
- commencer - start
- finir/terminer - finish
- marcher - walk
- écrire - write
- écouter - listen
- entendre - hear
- parler - speak/talk

- dire - say
- avoir - have
- pouvoir - to be able
- aller - to go
- étudier - study
- appeler - call
- donner - give
- envoyer - send
- lire - read
- demander - ask
- commander - order
- dire/raconter - tell
- prendre - take
- mettre - put
- toucher - touch
- penser - think
- arriver - arrive

- partir - leave/depart
- oublier - forget/leave
- se souvenir de - remember
- changer - change
- s'entraîner à/pratiquer - practice
- chercher - look for
- trouver - find
- voir - see
- rencontrer - meet
- apprendre - learn
- essayer - try
- ouvrir - open
- fermer - close

Discourse Markers (Marquers du discours)

- d'accord / okay, ... - okay...
- d'accord / ça va, ... - right
- écoute, ... - look, ... (listen)
- alors ... - so...
- enfin / soit, ... - anyway...

Conjunctions (conjonctions)

- aussi - also
- par exemple - for example
- peut-être - perhaps/maybe
- alors / donc - so/therefore
- même si - colloquial french for all three conjunctions: "even if", "even though" and "although"
    - même s'il fait beau, je ne pense pas que je vais y aller - even though/although the weather is nice, I do not think I am going to go
    - même si tu me donnais un million, je ne le mangerai pas - even if you gave me a million euros, I wouldn't eat it

- bien que - neutral/formal French for "even though" and "although"
    - bien qu'il y ait une présence policière, je ne me sens pas à l'aise ici - although there is a police presence, I do not feel comfortable here.

Sentence Adverbs (Locutions adverbiales)

- en fait, ... - actually...
- en gros, ... - basically...
- dans l'ensemble, ... - on the whole/generally

Adverbs of Frequency (Adverbes de fréquence)

- normalement - normally
- habituellement - usually
- souvent - often
- parfois - sometimes
- toujours - always
- jamais - never

Sequencers (Séquenceurs)

- premier / deuxième / troisième - first/second/third
- prochain - next
- dernier - last
- avant - before
- après - after
- ensuite - then
- jusqu'à - until

Appendix 2 - Cognates

[A2.1 - A2.14]

- -aire → -ary
    - un anniversaire - anniversary
    - l'adversaire - adversary
    - nécessaire - necessary
- -eux/euse → -ous
    - courageux - courageous
    - avantageux - advantageous
    - religieux - religious
- -ique → -ical
    - politique - political
    - électrique - electrical
    - pratique - practical
- -iste → -ist
    - un dentiste - dentist
    - un artiste - artist

- un linguiste - linguist

- -ant → -ing

    - choquant - shocking
    - intimidant - intimidating
    - ascendant - ascending

- -phie → -phy

    - la géographie - geography
    - la philosophie - philosophy
    - la discographie - discography

- -ier → -er

    - officier - officer
    - le prisonnier - prisoner
    - un charpentier - carpenter

- -ance → -ance

    - la distance - distance
    - l'ambulance - ambulance
    - la vengeance - vengeance

- -al → -al
  - central - central
  - musical - musical
  - local - local
- -ble → -ble
  - flexible - flexible
  - improbable - improbable
  - navigable - navigable
- -ct → -ct
  - correct - correct
  - impact - impact
  - aspect - aspect
- -ent → -ent
  - différent - different
  - l'accent - accent
  - innocent - innocent
- -ence → -ence

- intelligence - intelligence
- l'adolescence - adolescence
- la décadence - decadence

- -ical → -ique
  - identique - identical
  - magique - magical
  - logique - logical

Appendix 3 - False Friends

[A3.1 - A3.22]

- la commodité ≠ commodity (actual meaning- convenience)

    - le produit - commodity

    - Divers produits sont vendus sur les marchés mondiaux - Various products are sold on the world markets

- éventuellement ≠ eventually (actual meaning- possibly)

    - finalement - eventually

    - On a dû attendre, mais le bus est finalement arrivé - We had to wait, but the bus finally arrived

- basiquement ≠ basically

    - essentiellement/fondamentalement - basically

    - Le nouvel ordinateur est fondamentalement identique à l'ancien - The new computer is basically identical to the old one

- spécialement ≠ especially

    - en particulier - especially

- Beaucoup de touristes viennent ici, en particulier l'été - Many tourists come here, especially in the summer

- actuellement ≠ actually (actual meaning-currently)

  - en fait - actually

  - En fait, elle devrait porter la robe verte au lieu de la bleue - In fact, she should wear the green dress instead of the blue one

- la location ≠ location (actual meaning-rental)

  - un endroit - location

  - Ils ont trouvé un bel endroit pour construire leur maison - They found a nice place to build their home

- la discussion ≠ discussion (actual meaning-conversation)

  - un débat - debate

  - Le comité est parvenu à une décision après un long débat - The committee reached a decision after a long debate

- passer un examen ≠ to pass an exam (actual meaning-to take an exam)

  - réussir un examen - to pass an exam

- - Je dois réussir cet examen, si je veux étudier à l'étranger - I must pass this exam if I want to study abroad

- s'introduire ≠ to introduce (actual meaning-to penetrate/to insert)

  - se présenter - to introduce

  - Est-ce que tu peux te présenter, s'il te plaît ? - Can you introduce yourself, please?

- le caractère ≠ character (actual meaning-personality)

  - un personnage - character

  - Le personnage principal de ce film n'est pas très intéressant - The main character of this film is not very interesting

- excité ≠ excited (actual meaning-frantic; horny)

  - impatient de - excited

  - Je suis impatient de rencontrer mon correspondant - I am looking forward to meeting my correspondent

Appendix 4 - Verbs Using *Être* in the Perfect Tense

When forming the following verbs in the perfect tense, you should use *être* as the auxiliary verb instead of avoir. (E.g. *je suis allé*, not **j'ai allé*)

[A4.1 - A4.14]

- monter → je suis monté (went up)
- retourner → je suis retourné (returned)
- sortir → je suis sorti (went out)
- venir → je suis venu (came)
- arriver → je suis arrivé (arrived)
- naître → je suis né (was born)
- descendre → je suis descendu (went down)
- entrer → je suis entré (entered)
- rester → je suis resté (stayed)
- tomber → je suis tombé (fell)
- rentrer → je suis rentré (went back in)
- aller → je suis allé (went)

- mourir → je suis mort (died)
- partir → je suis parti (left)

Appendix 5 - Irregular Subjunctive Verbs

Most verbs follow a regular pattern in the subjunctive, but there are a few exceptions. Here are the most common ones:

[A5.1 - A5.9]

- faire - to do / to make
    - je fasse
    - tu fasses
    - il/elle/on fasse
    - nous fassions
    - vous fassiez
    - ils/elles fassent
- falloir - to be necessary
    - il faille
- pleuvoir - to rain
    - il pleuve
- pouvoir - to be able / can
    - je puisse

- tu puisses
- il/elle/on puisse
- nous puissions
- vous puissiez
- ils/elles puissent

- savoir - to know
    - je sache
    - tu saches
    - il/elle/on sache
    - nous sachions
    - vous sachiez
    - ils/elles sachent

- aller - to go
    - j'aille
    - tu ailles
    - il/elle/on aille
    - nous allions

- o vous alliez
- o ils/elles aillent

- avoir : to have
  - o j'aie
  - o tu aies
  - o il/elle/on ait
  - o nous ayons
  - o vous ayez
  - o ils/elles aient

- être : to be
  - o je sois
  - o tu sois
  - o il/elle/on soit
  - o nous soyons
  - o vous soyez
  - o ils/elles soient

- vouloir - to want

- je veuille
- tu veuilles
- il/elle/on veuille
- nous voulions
- vous vouliez
- ils/elles veuillent

Fin

More from Olly

If you have enjoyed this book, you will love all the other free language learning content I publish each week online.

My Blog

I Will Teach You A Language:
http://www.iwillteachyoualanguage.com

Podcast

The I Will Teach You A Language Podcast

iPhone: http://www.iwillteachyoualanguage.com/itunes

Android: http://www.iwillteachyoualanguage.com/stitcherradio

Find me on social media

Facebook: http://www.facebook.com/iwillteachyoualanguage

Twitter: http://www.twitter.com/olly_iwtyal

Thank You for Reading

I hope you have enjoyed this book and that your French has improved as a result! A lot of hard work went into creating this book, and if you would like to support me, the best way to do so would be with an honest review on the Amazon store. This helps other people find the book and lets them know what to expect.

To do this:

    1. Visit http://www.amazon.com

    2. Click "Your Account" in the menu bar

    3. Click "Your Orders" from the drop-down menu

    4. Select this book from the list and leave an honest review!

Thank you for your support!

    - Olly Richards

Printed in Poland
by Amazon Fulfillment
Poland Sp. z o.o., Wrocław